T0157577

VERITAS

A Dream Catcher Journal for Organizational Change

FELICITY MC CANN

BALBOA.
PRESS

A DIVISION OF HAY HOUSE

Balboa Press books may be ordered through booksellers or by contacting:

Balboa Press
A Division of Hay House
1663 Liberty Drive
Bloomington, IN 47403
www.balboapress.com.au
1 (877) 407-4847

Print information available on the last page.

ISBN: 978-1-5043-0653-9 (sc)
ISBN: 978-1-5043-0654-6 (e)

Balboa Press rev. date: 02/08/2017

Dedicated to the Seeker of Truth

Contents

INTRODUCTION

Each of us have many aspects to our personalities which we adopt as the need arises, whether it is the personality of the good girl or boy, the mother, father, teacher, loving son or daughter, caring wife or husband, reliable employee, best friend, loving sister or brother or the doting grandparent.

In our dreams we see the many facets of our personality reflected back to us through the dreaming mind and we are forced to accept the negative emotions, as well as the virtues of our own personalities, if we wish to grow as a soul.

We also learn from renowned psychologists such as Freud and Jung, that in our subconscious mind we each possess many complexes that influence our behaviour in relation to other people and also in how we view ourselves.

Complexes according to Freud, such as an inferiority complex, an Oedipus complex, a megalomaniac complex, a vertigo complex, an agoraphobic complex, angry young man complex, not good enough complex; the list is endless, but each one of these complexes can take over, or dominate our conscious mind and behaviour for a period of time.

And according to Jung, the archetypes of the collective unconscious such as the Trickster, the Shadow, the Ego, the Anima and Animus, the Wise old Man and the Wise old Woman can also take over the conscious mind at any one time.

In the search to become a complete person, we need to

recognise and acknowledge these aspects of our own personality and we can do this through various techniques that operate in modern psychotherapy, that reduce the buffers we have, that prevent recognition of our more undesirable traits, or we can use our dreams.

Whichever way we choose to do it, hard work and persistence will be required and it will also require courage to be able to look oneself squarely in the eye and admit, that yes, I am like that.

It is only when we have reached a point in our psychological and emotional development, that the subconscious mind will bring to our conscious mind through dreams, the various aspects of our personalities that need to be addressed.

As the saying goes, "When the student is ready, the teacher will appear."

This saying is particularly relevant to me, as being an Irish school teacher in an Independent school in New South Wales, Australia; I found that my dreams were urging me to take on a culture of bullying and harassment that existed within the school in which I taught.

For evil to flourish, it is only necessary for good men to do nothing.

CHAPTER ONE

THE NORTHERN IRELAND EXPERIENCE

My Irish background, similar to that of the Australian Aborigine, (The Irish are often referred to, as the Aborigine of the North), enables me to access helpful information from family members who have passed on, as well as providing vital information similar to that of a vision quest, to keep me safe and provide for my material and emotional needs.

My Irish pagan origins that Christianity has never been able to fully eradicate, still ties me to the land through a reverence that I have for the medicinal use of herbs and plant life and a belief in the power of the Goddess, that has simply been transferred to Mary, as well as a belief in the unseen forces of Magic and nature, the natural and the supernatural, including fairies and the little people.

The pagan tradition of wearing an amulet for protection while travelling away from home has become Christianized into the wearing of a St. Christopher medal.

The pagan rites that included symbols of the four elements can be found in the ceremonies of the Catholic Church.

Flowers representing the earth are placed on the altar, incense representing air, a candle representing fire, and water.

The pagan rite of cleansing before entering an abode has also been usurped and is symbolised by the holy water at the front of the church, which all use to make the sign of the cross to cleanse of ill feelings, before entering the house of God.

The traditional Gaelic greeting in Donegal that I learned from my Gaelic teacher in school has always been in the form of a blessing and has also been incorporated into the rites of the Catholic Church.

It is no accident that the Irish way of life and the pagan traditions of the Irish, have had a huge impact on Christianity, given that there were innumerable Irish missionaries sent out across the world.

Several of my aunts were missionary sisters and my grandmother's older sister only met her youngest sister for the first time, when she too was sent to Calcutta as a missionary sister.

One of my grandmother's daughters, named Alice, continued this tradition and was sent as a Nazereth missionary sister to Kenya and my father also had an Aunt named Jane and a sister, whose noviciate name was Gabriel, who were missionary sisters as well.

The cross is a pagan, cosmic symbol of the tree of life, dating back thousands of years before the birth of Christ, connecting heaven and earth, the vertical arm representing spirituality and the horizontal arm representing the earth.

Christianity however, also usurped this symbol so that it has now become synonymous the death of Christ.

The Celtic cross includes the solar disc around the arms of the cross, to represent the sun and eternity and together they represented the earth and the revolution of the four seasons, but the cross was often used for luck, as well as protection.

The gypsies viewed the cross as a masculine symbol (phallus) and the circle as a feminine symbol (yoni) and so the solar cross, represented sexual union.

A custom of painting a cross on the right foreleg of a horse and a circle on the left foreleg was believed to create a magical hobble to stop the horse from running away. This tradition was based on the theory that the two symbols would attract each other as in the magical practice of, like attracts like, and so draw the two feet together and prevent the animal from straying.

Many of the pagan feast days and natural festivals of the seasons became Saint's days and festivals of the Christian Church, in an attempt to try extinguish their pagan origins.

The tradition in Ireland of including the name Mary for boys, born in the month of May, retains remnants of the fertility Shabbat in the Irish calendar acknowledging the coming together of the Goddess and God.

Also the Lammas Fair, held at the beginning of August in many towns in Ireland, is simply a continuation of the celebration of the pagan Harvest festival.

The inclusion of the name 'Mary' as a boy's name is not without its drawbacks however.

One wet, rainy night during "The Troubles "in Northern Ireland, I was stopped by the British Armed Forces, whilst driving from one town to another, when an amusing incident occurred, which provided a sense of light relief, to what could have been an intimidating situation.

When the car was flagged down by the British soldier in charge of the operation and we came to a halt, orders were barked at me and my two passengers to get out of the car and line up against a wall, a common occurrence in Northern Ireland at the time.

One member of the group of soldiers, who were all dressed in combat fatigues and carrying rifles, demanded to know where we were going, what our names were and demanded proof of identification.

I produced my driver's licence as ordered and stated my name.

My two passengers, who were brothers, were both born in the month of May.

The elder brother stated his name as Mary Dermot O' Connell and the second brother gave his name as Mary Seamus O' Connell.

"Funny", the solder remarked with a snort of derision, as he muttered some inaudible remark to his companions while pointing his gun menacingly at the older brother, and harshly demanded proof of identification, in a tone of voice that brooked no argument.

To his incredulous belief, both brothers duly did so and handed over identification papers which the British soldier painstakingly scrutinized in the pouring rain, with the help of the low beam of a hand held torch and then eventually with a resentful snarl, handed the identification papers back and curtly told us to get in the car and be on our way.

The practice of incorporating a carving of a Sheila-na-gig, a little naked woman, squatting and exposing her vagina, into the cornerstone of old Irish Churches, has ensured that the tradition of the Goddess will never be completely eradicated by Christianity.

This is similar to the bas-relief in St. Andrews Anglican Cathedral in Sydney, where a depiction of Moses wearing horns has been carved and is located at the rear of the altar.

The Old Testament tells us that Moses was transformed after encountering God (really the Goddess) at the burning bush and so the horns representing the consort of the Goddess have been ascribed to him by the sculptor, to signify his transformation.

The Italian sculptor, who had been commissioned to carve the bas-relief, had apparently completed the sculpture before the inclusion of horns had been discovered.

It is a magnificent piece of work that, though thought provoking, is definitely worth a look.

I find myself smiling every time I think of how the sculptor managed to pull off this coup.

Chapter Two

The Curse of the Irish.

Ireland has often been referred to as, The Land of Saints and Scholars, because of the disproportionate number of nuns and clergy who have emanated from its shores, as well as the inordinate number of authors, playwrights and poets who have made a sizable contribution to the world of literature and theatre.

Nostradamus noted that the Irish were an honourable race, but unfortunately were too fond of the potato. In other words, the alcohol made from the potato, affected their outlook on life, creating a sentimentality that did not always serve them well.

Irish poet and playwright Oscar Wilde once described the Irish as "a nation of great failures, but the greatest talkers since the Greeks."

Interestingly enough, the Irish and the Greeks are more similar to each other, than any other culture, according to one renowned Anthropologist.

The Irish are quick to acknowledge that alcohol does play a considerable part in their culture and a pub visit is a must for any tourist. The imbibing of one or two glasses of alcohol tends to encourages a loquaciousness that might not otherwise be as forthcoming.

Ironically in 2014, The Sunday Telegraph in Australia reported that a school in South Korea refused a teaching position to an Irish school teacher, informing her that they had a policy of not employing the Irish because they are all drunks.

This is a sad, but true indictment, of a number of Irish people.

One of my father's older brothers was an alcoholic, and though a charming individual, he had a lonely life that was wasted through lack of ambition and drive, because of his addiction to alcohol and for this reason my father decided to take "The pledge", forswearing off alcohol for the rest of his life.

It is probably one of life's little ironies that despite being an alcoholic and living what may have appeared to others to be a miserable life, this particular uncle, managed to outlive my father and another brother, by more than a decade.

I myself have been born with addictive tendencies and a line on the palm of my left hand, serves as a testimony to this, fortunately the same mark is not a feature of the palm of my right hand and so all addictive tendencies can be overcome.

Also, despite a certain amount of overindulgence in my early life, I was fortunate enough to marry an Australian who didn't drink and as drinking alone has never appealed to me, it was not difficult to dramatically reduce and restrict alcohol intake, even on social occasions.

The dreaming mind will support our efforts to improve our lives. It is like having your own personal Cheer Leader and my dreams informed me that I had managed to access the gold within, from my relationships with my husband and my two sons.

A great deal of Irish alcoholism stems I believe, from the Christianization of the Irish people.

An unnatural and unhealthy attitude to sex, as well as a manipulation of the Irish people through guilt, created a fanatical approach to modesty and sex which resulted in an over indulgence in alcohol to relieve emotional and sexual frustration.

Sigmund Freud, the famous psychiatrist, claimed that sexual

frustration and sexual problems lay at the root of most of our psychological problems. The Irish may prove him right!

However the Irish culture is a spiritual culture and like the Australian Aborigine, the voices of our ancestors speak to us in our dreams, a talent that has managed to rescue me from many a tight spot or untenable position.

CHAPTER THREE

A CALL TO ACTION

The subconscious mind continually processes information that our conscious mind maybe unaware of and the dreaming mind will bring this information into our dreams, to alert the dreamer to circumstances that they are either ignoring, or to warn the dreamer that the they are heading in a direction that is not in the dreamer's best interests.

One particular night I had a dream showing me "The Writing on the Wall "as in the biblical story of the Old Testament, I knew that it was a warning that my life was about to change and unfortunately not for the better.

Sure enough, not long after that, the Principal of the Independent school that I was teaching in, with the collusion of its Board of Governors, terminated my employment illegally, despite my lifetime tenure, in order to silence my protestations about bullying and harassment that existed within the school.

The beginning of the end began, after I sent an official letter of complaint to the Principal, at the start of the new school year, in order to draw her attention to the systematic bullying and harassment in the school and by the end of that same year, I had been suspended from my employment and by the middle of the following year, my position at the school was illegally terminated without my consent and based on deliberate deception by the Principal of the school.

The letter which appeared to initiate this chain of events, clearly documented the systematic bullying and an accurate record of dates and times substantiated what was said.

The bullying I experienced was I believe, also due in part to my participation in a Teacher's march after which I was quoted in an article in a respectable newspaper, as advocating the need for teachers to stand up for their rights and the school in which I taught, was also named.

That was a big mistake!

Once you draw attention to yourself, you become a target.

Ironically, I had been trailing at the back of the Teacher's march as I had really only gone to give support to the Union Representative at the time, who happened to be a personal friend of mine and as I would not have considered myself to be a militant individual, I stayed with the stragglers at the back of the march.

The fact that at the time it was the Chinese year of the Dragon and I was sporting a red T-shirt, with a dragon emblazoned on the front, must have caught the eye of the Journalist and prompted her to quiz me about my reasons for marching.

When I returned to school the next day, there was a lot of whispering in little groups and covert glances were furtively cast in my direction, which made me feel decidedly uneasy.

Eventually someone asked me if I had spoken to a reporter at the march, to which I replied that someone had asked if I minded giving them my reasons for marching and so I did.

However, there it was next day in the newspaper, a little paragraph in the third column giving my name and school and my reasons for marching.

I could feel resentment from other staff members that I had been singled out for this little bit of notoriety, as I was not the 'Official spokesperson' and who was I to give an opinion?

But we play the hand that fate deals us, whether good or bad.

The irony of the timing of this situation was not lost on me, as the day following the march was my birthday and I had no doubt that someone in spirit had provided this opportunity for me.

Most likely it was my father wishing me a "Happy Birthday", or it could have been my great uncle Bernard on my mother's side, who had been a journalist for a Boston newspaper in America.

The Irish believe that the dead look after the living and around anniversary time and on birthday occasions, the dead put an opportunity the way of the living.

But whichever one it was who sent me this opportunity, they set my feet on the road to change.

This incident, combined with the letter and a Thesis on organizational change, that I had given the new Principal to read, that I had written as part of a requirement into a Masters program at University, and which had documented the state of uproar that existed in the school at that time and the problems associated with going Co-educational, could also have been a problem, as once again, who was I to comment on what was happening?

Despite having permission from the Principal at the time to carry out my action research with a number of the teaching staff, the information gathered and the insight gleaned about the unhappy state and feelings of powerlessness, that the staff articulated in the action research, clearly ear- marked me not only as a reformist, but a whistle blower as well, not a good position to be in. However, that was not the end of the story, nor was it the beginning, but somewhere in-between.

Not only did the Board of Governors and the school principal collude to sack me for threatening to expose the culture of bullying that existed within the school, but a deliberate campaign was waged against me, to prevent me from ever teaching again.

It is necessary to point out to the reader, that personal ethics are not the same as business ethics, and that is why individuals like me, naively believe that we are all working for the greater good, when in fact an organization is only working to maintain a lucrative bottom line and maintaining a certain Persona to the world, in order to keep that lucrative bottom line.

It is therefore necessary to remember that all Organizations are Organizations first and foremost; everything else is of secondary importance.

CHAPTER FOUR

LIFE IS STRANGER THAN FICTION

It was impossible for me to secure a lawyer who would represent my case, because of a fear of intimidation from the powerful Board of Governors of the Independent school, whose connections reached all echelons of society, and who could possibly threaten their livelihood if they did so.

Several lawyers I approached were apologetic and declined my case, while one who initially took up my case, withdrew a short time later after pressure was brought to bear upon him.

This particular lawyer had represented my case to apply for an Apprehended Violence Order, also known as an A.V.O., against a teacher's aide at the school, who had been harassing me on behalf of the principal of the school.

However, on the day that we were in Court, just as the person accused of harassing me was asked to take the stand, a letter, the contents of which I was not privy to, was passed to my lawyer, which he glanced at briefly, before handing it to the sitting Judge. After reading the letter, the Judge asked me to stand and when I did, with my heart pounding in my chest from anxiety, I became rooted to the spot in horror, as the Judge addressed me in a scathing manner and accused me of being a trouble maker and dismissed my case.

My lawyer paid lip service to being horrified by the Judge's decision, and had my case transferred to the District Court. The lawyer then withdrew his services as he did not want to subpoena individuals, who had witnessed the bullying and harassment that I had suffered at the hands of this individual and that aroused my suspicions. Also, the fact that the Judge in the previous Court had dismissed out of hand, other physical evidence that was available to substantiate the need for legal intervention, clearly indicated a breach in his duty of care, as well as a distinct lack of impartially.

It was only later that I realised that the in-house drama in the Court room, was to discredit me locally, and to avoid any sympathetic support for my cause and to keep the proceedings veiled in a cloak of secrecy by having it transferred to the District Court in the City.

I was mortified by what had happened in the Court room as it had been 'a packed house', and to top it all, the victory shout of 'Yes' from my harasser, as she punched the air with both fists, completely took the wind out of sails, as I realised that she had been aware all along of what was going to happen in Court.

It took me quite long time to come to terms with what happened in the Court, and to get over the huge disappointment I felt with the Justice system.

In my dreams, I dreamed that I was going to Court to give evidence against someone who had hit my grandmother with their car.

I dreamed that the Court-room was an old fashioned Court-room, in the colours of black and white, just like in the old movies on the television screen.

In the dream I was asked to take the witness stand, but I felt really nervous about taking the stand and I was frightened that I would not be able to testify because of my nervousness.

I prayed to God in desperation, to help me not to be nervous as

I was determined to testify at how badly injured my grandmother had been by the car and how much pain she was in.

In the witness box, I began to describe the unbearable pain that my grandmother suffered from, that ran up and down the left side of her body and how severe it was and as I described the pain, I could feel the excruciating pain myself and I woke up.

The fact that this dream was in black and white, illustrates the black and white attitude that I have regarding right and wrong.

The old fashioned Court-room is an indication that my values appear to be outdated in today's society, where the system of the "old school tie" allows powerful organizations and institutions to make up their own rules and affect the outcome of a case, regardless of its merits.

To dream of praying, is an indication that strenuous efforts are required on the part of the dreamer, if they wish to avoid failure.

A car in a dream represents the individual whose actions injured the grandmother aspect of my nature, which like the wise old woman of Jungian psychology, is working for the greater good and is a source of growth and vitality.

My acute sense of justice and fair play spurred me on, to continue to fight and I began to buy as many second-hand Law books, as I could find and I read them with a passion.

My dreams would provide me with a clue as to which angle to take and I wrote reams and reams of information that would eventually be culled down to one or two points only.

To convince myself that I was capable of representing myself, I decided that it would like arguing in a debate; only I had much more to lose.

I had not however, bargained on the overwhelming experience of going into the District Court to represent myself and when it was my turn to speak, I burst into tears as the enormity of my situation suddenly dawned on me.

The Judge however, was extremely kind and asked those not involved in the case, to leave the Court room.

A few moments later, after the Court had been cleared, the Judge asked me to explain my case.

Unfortunately, I was so crippled with nerves; I had difficulty in articulating clearly why I was there.

However, a fortunate incident happened, that provided an opportunity for me to regain my composure slightly and allowed me to fight another day.

The legal representative of the teacher's aide, who was provided by the Board of the Independent school, was a young American Lawyer, who put in an objection that he had not been properly briefed about my case and certain information that I was alluding to, was not in his portfolio.

The Judge then looked in my direction and advised me that he would postpone the case to another day, to enable me to send the young lawyer all of the information pertaining to the case and with that concluded the proceedings.

Not surprisingly, I was delighted with the opportunity to send the young lawyer all my evidence, as judging by what had already happened in the previous Court, I had no doubt that he had been given a watered down version of the facts.

Sure enough at the next Court sitting, his demeanour was friendlier and he almost seemed to be trying to coach me in my responses, but alas, I was not well enough versed in legal jargon and I was badly frustrated by my inability to understand what he was alluding to.

The court case was once again adjourned to another day and this time the young American lawyer had been replaced by a female lawyer who appeared to have no qualms with the way the Principal of the Independent school had manipulated the facts to her own advantage.

When I decided that I was going to have to represent myself at the District Court, I discovered that the case number had been changed and so I wrote a letter to the Principal Registrar at the District Court, as not only had the number been changed, but the correspondence that I received from the District Court, seemed to indicate I was the person whom the A.V.O. had been taken out against.

The Principal Registrar at the time quickly responded to my concerns and assured me that it was standard procedure to change the case file number for administrative purposes, because of the change in jurisdiction.

Later however, when I lost my case and was ordered to pay costs, the number of the case cited on the respondent's legal bill was the original case number.

When I rang the Legal firm about the matter, the respondents' lawyer casually suggested that perhaps an A.V.O. had been taken out against me the complainant, to which I responded; 'I was never informed of anything like that'.

In fact I was to discover later, that this was another dirty tactic of the Board of Governors of the Independent school.

Information was filed without my knowledge and the failure to follow due legal process by the Independent school was it seemed, sanctioned by the Courts.

Another local lawyer, whom I had approached, had once been a student at the school in question, and had the audacity to charge me $300 to simply tell me in an arrogant fashion, that I didn't have a case.

Fortunately, I had a dream the night before the appointment, showing me that the principal of the school had gotten to him first, so his words fell on deaf ears.

It also seemed, according to a telephone technician, that my phone had been tapped. I had contacted him regarding concerns about a strange click that I could hear in the ear piece, just as I picked up my phone and a similar click, at the conclusion of a conversation, before I returned my phone to its cradle and his assessment of the situation was that my phone was tapped.

The phone company that I was registered with also caused me a lot of unnecessary hardship later, when my final phone bill was incorrectly addressed, despite the accurate delivery of all previous bills.

I only learned of this mistake when I had phoned the operator with a query on another matter, and was casually informed by her, that an unpaid phone bill had been sent to a debt collector.

I was stunned by this latest piece of information and said that I had been with the company for twenty years and had always paid my phone bills.

The operator said that I had failed to pay the last bill.

When I requested the date of the bill in question, I realised that I had not received that particular bill and asked her to forward it to me.

It was too late she said, as it had already been given to a debt collector.

I immediately contacted the Ombudsman and the Privacy Commissioner and complained about the lack of cooperation from the phone company in question.

Later, when the debt collector contacted me for payment, I had already received advice from both the Ombudsman and the Privacy Commissioner and demanded to know the address on the phone bill.

The information he gave me, confirmed that the bill had been incorrectly addressed and to my surprise, the date on the phone bill, was prior to the date of the latest bill which I had paid.

After much heated discussion about the misdirected mail, the debt collector informed me that he would not pursue this debt any further.

The telephone technician's observation about the clicking noises in my phone I believe, explained my inability to secure an interview for any of the multitude of employment opportunities that I applied for.

One potential employer that I spoke to from another city regarding the possibility of marketing Reading Material in schools, was extremely enthusiastic that I join his team when he became aware of my professional background and at the conclusion of our conversation, said that he would post a sample of the material the same day and that he would contact me again a few days later.

As promised, I received the sample of Reading Material which I still have, but I never heard from him again and my calls went unanswered, as they did to so many other potential employers.

At the office of a Welfare job provider, that I was eventually forced to contact due to my reduced financial circumstances, the representative deliberately embarrassed me by publicly disparaging my ability to get even bar work because of my age, despite having had previous experience of working in bars, both in Manchester and London in the U.K.

The local police and the Judiciary were also unlawfully influenced by the mighty power of the Board Members of this Independent school.

My Legal application to the local Court to get an A.V.O. against the Principal of the school to stop her campaign of harassment and bullying, was doctored by the Court clerks in a disparaging fashion and my name was written as "Sod you McCann" and my date of birth registered as that of a new born baby to make the application null and void.

When I brought this to the attention of the sitting Judge, he asked me if I would like to include this deliberate interference in my application to Court and on affirming that I would like to do so, the case was adjourned for two weeks.

When we returned to Court, the original Judge had been replaced by another Judge, who dismissed my application, and as casually as that, the case was terminated.

This was not an isolated occurrence, as sympathetic Judges were replaced by others who were less sympathetic and games were played regarding times and dates of Court appearances and information that the Court granted access to, was difficult to obtain.

In the District Court, subpoenas that had been served were disallowed and as a result I lost that case from lack of concrete proof and had to pay costs for the other party, which was a bitter pill to swallow.

In his book, *The Justice Game*, Geoffrey Robertson, who is in actual fact an internationally-famous barrister, illustrates that the administration of justice can depend upon a fortunate turn of events, the personalities of the judges and juries, as well as other random factors.

Also in his book, regarding telling the truth in law, we are made aware that we should never presume that someone obviously well qualified in that discipline, will present the truth of a situation, whether in reference to facts, or in expressing opinions based on facts.

The latter was certainly true of the school principal and the legal representative of the Independent school, in all the legal undertakings regarding my situation.

Chapter Five

Cats

I began to dream of cats a great deal during this period.

A cat represents ill luck and usually refers to a female, (a dog in a dream traditionally represents a male), and if you are unable to kill the cat, or get rid of it in the dream and the cat attacks you, the dream is a warning that you have enemies, who will go to great lengths and any extreme to cause you lose of property.

I found this dream quite nerve racking as it indicated that serious trouble was around me and that I needed to be, frighteningly careful.

One dream of a fluffy blue cat that deliberately bit my thumb and which I hurled out onto the road, as a huge truck was bearing down towards me, represented the female teacher's aide, who was having problems in her personal life and so was feeling blue, represented by the fluffy blue cat and who had lied about me in school and in Court and whose costs I had to pay.

A thumb in a dream represents your personal power and when someone or thing, injures your thumb, they have affected your ability to do something. This was the case here, the person had deliberately prevented me from getting justice by failing to tell the truth about a situation, and the untruths were then manipulated and used to discredit my character and eventually sack me.

This particular staff member was also psychologically living on a knife edge and her volatile temper had been vitriolic towards a number of staff members and now she allowed herself to become a pawn in the hands of the Principal, as did another male staff member, who had a dubious track record in his teaching career and had who been transferred to our school under suspicious circumstances.

These two unhappy individuals who had personal problems of their own, now became the centre of attention and were 'protected' by the establishment for the part that they were going to play in ridding the Principal of an unwanted individual, who had become a thorn in her side.

My dream of prawns one night was merely a pun for the word pawns and confirmed for me, that these two individuals had allowed themselves to be used in the unsavoury shenanigans of the school Principal.

The fact that the Independent school paid for legal representation for these two individuals, despite one being a teacher's aide and the other, a teacher of questionable attitude, was an indication of the lengths that the school was prepared to go to, in order to silence me.

Another dream of a mewing white cat caused even more grave concern, as it indicated that some false friend was using all the words and work at their disposal to do me harm.

A clean white cat also indicates entanglements, which seemingly harmless, would be a source of sorrow and would cause financial hardship.

The female teacher's aide, who had been having marital problems, began to attend my regular dancing classes and attached herself to me, like a limpet on a rock, shadowing my every move and even following me when I went to the bathroom, making me feel decidedly uneasy.

Uncomfortable as this situation was, I reluctantly endured her behaviour, as she had complained so bitterly about her unhappy domestic life. However, when she began to verbally abuse me in front of my fellow class mates and a note of jealousy began to creep into her conversations about my friendship with a male companion, which then escalated to abusive phone calls to my home and accusations of avoiding her, that turned even nastier, when she began to brag about how my male companion was interested in her, I began to worry about her mental state.

I mentioned the situation to my male companion, a widower and a shameless flirt and suggested that he tread carefully, or he may find himself cited in a divorce case.

The gentleman in question, and I am using this term very loosely, did heed my advice, but this unfortunately, only exacerbated the situation more and culminated in a complete melt down of the staff member in question.

One evening, at the venue where my dancing lessons were held, the teacher's aide went up to the reception desk and in front of the long queue of individuals, of which I was one, who were waiting to pay for their dancing lesson, she turned around to face the queue and looking directly at me, she began to shout in a loud voice,

"You are a shit Felicity, nothing but a shit and I hate you", and then as the line of stunned dancers watched, me included, she walked from the front of the queue to the back of the room and exited through a side door.

The final straw came when she began to scream at me in front of a clerk in the school library. The clerk looked really frightened and I had the distinct impression that she herself may have been subjected to the same kind of verbal abuse in the past and the shocked expression on her face indicated that she was horrified, that this teacher's aide had the audacity to publically abuse one of the teaching staff.

I said to her, "You are a witness to what has happened here", but in a terrified voice she said, "Don't involve me."

Then there was a strange turn of events.

The teacher's aide who had appeared to be so overwrought and out of control a few minutes previously, suddenly announced that she was going to see the Principal, and catching both the clerk and myself off guard, she dashed out of the library and rushed off to the principal's office.

After getting over the surprise of what had just happened, I decided that I had better go and see the Principal as well, to explain my version of what had happened and the events leading up to it.

The Principal, a shrewish looking individual with a long patrician nose, could size up a situation in one second flat, and had been sent as a trouble shooter to the school, to get rid of staff that had been and still were a problem for the public image of the Independent school.

When she had first arrived three years previously, the Principal had taken the unusual step of having an interview with each individual staff member, with the intention of information gathering about the school and other staff members and as a result of these private little meetings, there were several job reshuffles.

In my interview, the Principal surprised me by mentioning the name of one of my sisters and was unflattering in her comments about her.

This surprised me at the time, as I could see no relevance to what my sister did and to my employment as a teacher.

What the Principal did disclose by these comments, was the way in which the Independent School takes a personal interest in the lives of its staff members and their family connections.

Overtones of 'Big Brother' were definitely at work here. Despite the Principle appearing to lend a sympathetic and understanding ear to my account of events, there was a bizarre twist to the situation.

Suddenly the teacher's aide was being chaperoned around the school by another school clerk, (not the one who had witnessed the event surprisingly enough) and conspiratorial looks were cast in my direction and I was beginning to sense that something was not quite right.

Individual teachers would try and engage me in conversation about the teacher's aide, but I had been warned by the Principal not to say anything until the situation had been investigated.

Had I only realized that this ploy by the Principal guaranteed my silence and enabled her to set a chain of events in motion, that would prevent the truth from getting out, I would not have such a willing participant in my own downfall.

Initially a meeting was arranged for me with a member of the School Board, to supposedly investigate my claims of bullying and harassment.

I was surprised to learn that the meeting was scheduled to take place in an old weatherboard cottage that was located on school grounds, and that was situated away from the main building, instead of in one of the modern, brightly lit rooms, usually used for meetings in the school proper.

It was only afterwards, that I realized that the reason this particular room was used, was to keep the meeting private and away from the prying eyes of other staff members.

This secrecy was to set the tone for all my interactions with both the Principal and the School Board.

It was not by accident that I discovered that a copy of the book; *For the Term of His Natural Life* by Marcus Clarke, had been deliberately left on my desk by some unknown person.

This book deals with the interaction between those who wield power and those who suffer and this is illustrated through the wrongful imprisonment of the hero Rufus Dawes.

Also, the book was stamped with the name of a school where I had taught many years previously and served as a reminder to me, of the extensive connections of those on the Independent school's Board.

I could not help but wonder if this was a supportive touch by a friend, or a spiteful touch from an enemy. I decided that the latter was the more likely judging by the sequence of events that followed.

On the appointed day and at the appointed time, I arrived at the designated place with a yellow Manilla folder under my arm.

The slim, dark haired, female representative from the Board of the Independent school, was dressed in corporate attire, and was already in the appointed room and was seated at a large, dark brown, old fashioned dining room table that was slightly worse for wear and which was now beginning its second life as a conference table. The business-like young woman stood up to greet me in an officious, but pleasant manner and invited me to sit down at the table.

With a feeling of eager anticipation that everything would be speedily resolved to everyone's satisfaction, I sat down at the table and the charade began.

The Representative began to read from a document, the list of grievances that I had brought to the attention of the school principal. The Representative asked me to confirm that the contents of the list were correct.

I agreed that the list was indeed correct and as I did so, I opened up the folder that I had brought with me and added that I had evidence to support what I said.

Suddenly the young woman seemed to lose her composure and began to hurriedly gather up the files that she had brought with her and told me in a curt voice, that she needed to adjourn the meeting to another time, as she was not prepared.

And on that brief note, she quickly exited the room and left me feeling quite perplexed as to what was going on.

It is important to note here that a second meeting to address my concerns was never rescheduled.

Years of teaching, involving the maintaining of a daily journal, as well as the daily recording of my dreams, had enabled me to have an accurate account of times, dates and places where incidents had taken place and this unexpected documented information, had taken the Representative completely by surprise.

I would advise everyone to keep a daily account of the day's happenings, as you never know when the small amount of time and effort required doing this, will pay dividends.

It is with this view in mind that I have included a section at the back of this book to enable the reader to do just that.

After this fiasco of a meeting, even close friends on teaching staff began to avoid me and on a couple of occasions, two male teachers behaved in an unprofessional manner by coming into my classroom unannounced and ignoring my presence as teacher in charge, began to make announcements to the students.

Then, when students began to tell me about one particular teacher openly discussing me in class, alarm bells began to ring and I knew that something needed to be done to stop this insidious behaviour.

When I challenged this male teacher's behaviour in the staffroom, other staff members were horrified to hear the teacher involved, begin to brag about how much he enjoyed embarrassing a particular student in my class because she was on medication for anxiety, as if his inappropriate behaviour towards me, was nothing compared to what he did to the students.

I immediately reported his behaviour to the Principal.

By now the reader will have an idea of what was going to happen.

Both the teacher's aide and this particular teacher became the two pawns used by the Principal to fabricate evidence, to enable the School Board to sack me illegally for being a whistle blower.

Chapter Six

Games People Play

J ustice disappeared and instead a reign of terror replaced it and eventually after years of not understanding how this situation could be allowed to happen, a Judge in the Federal Magistrate's Court, informed me that I had been constructively dismissed from my position.

The downsizing of my teaching position in school and my relegation to an isolated and unimportant roll on the teaching staff sent a clear message to other staff members that I was a problem in some unidentified way.

This course of action is typical of the middle management of an organization, who fears the legitimacy, or validity of accusations levelled at its door, and especially by someone from the lower echelons of the organization.

There is a fear that the individual may be voicing concerns already held by others and will create a situation, which will cause those in power, to question the effectiveness of those in middle management and so defamation is used by middle management, to blackmail a whistle blower into submission and convince any sympathisers, that the person has deceived them.

Six months after I had made the Principal aware of my concerns, I was accused of the exact behaviour that I had complained about and despite requesting to view my professional file, the Principal informed me that she had thrown it out and so I was unable to access any information and so defend myself against these deliberately contrived falsehoods.

When the idea of procedural fairness is loosely banded about to create an impression of integrity and honour in dealing with situations, please do not make the mistake that I made and assume that working in an Independent school, will include that right. It does not!

Independent and Private schools are not held accountable as is State, or Public schools.

They are not required to report on unacceptable behaviour either, by its teaching staff, or by its students.

And the media has frequently gone to great lengths to remind us of this fact, with the innumerable cases of child abuse and paedophilia that it has exposed, in its relentless search for justice.

Justice however, can be as elusive as a butterfly and just when it appears to be within reach, it flutters off beyond your grasp, tantalizingly close, but not close enough.

A distant family member who had taught with me for many years at this school, (Independent schools are notorious for nepotism), chose to believe the distortion of events and fabricated instances of misconduct that middle management resorted to and instead of checking the veracity of what was said about me, contacted a close family member and persuaded her that I was delusional and needed help. This family member then contacted the local Hospital and feigning a concern for my welfare, tried to have me sectioned under the Mental Health Act.

It still puzzles me as to why this close family member did what they did and I suppose I will never know.

The distant relative also told staff members at the school, that the school had offered me $50,000 dollars in compensation, but that I had refused to take it.

I was stunned when I heard this, as it was news to me.

What the school had offered me was a year's paid leave while they said; they would investigate the situation and which I knew was a ploy to get me out of the school quietly, with a view to terminating my position, a course of action that they had taken with several other teachers in the past.

They had also offered me a teaching position in another location which was several hours distant from where I lived, on condition that I didn't tell anyone what had happened.

Based on the behaviour of the Principal regarding the situation at the time and the subsequent witch hunt, carried out by the representative of the School Board regarding my complaints, I declined both offers and so I was informed by the Head of the Union whose help I had sought, that I was not to return to the school, as I had been suspended without pay until further notice.

The Spokesperson for the Union played a sorry role in this affair.

When I had first contacted the Union, I had spoken to a young woman who was seriously concerned about what was happening at the school and she advised me to make the school aware that the Union was now involved in the situation, which I duly did.

This young woman was later replaced by a more mature member of the Union, who came to the school to meet with both the Principal and myself.

This lady was really efficient and managed to quickly get negotiations about the situation underway.

However, I believe she was too good at what she did and so she too was replaced after she discovered that the school had fabricated a meeting between her, the School Board and me, because in reality, she had no knowledge of the meeting. The intention of the school Principal was to waylay me and terminate my employment without the Union representative's knowledge.

Fortunately, on the morning of the supposed meeting, when a secretary laid a note on my desk as she casually informed me that the Union Representative had sent a message advising me about a meeting in the Principal's office, I smelt a rat, and phoned the Union Representative to confirm the information.

The Union Representative could barely contain her anger and warned me not to go the meeting, as she had no knowledge of it.

When the bell rang for change of class, instead of going to the charade of a meeting, I simply went to my classroom.

As an experienced school teacher, I am aware of the necessity of getting the attention of the class as quickly as possible to maintain order in the classroom and so it has always been my habit to say a prayer at the beginning of each class, a strategy I learned from my Irish school days.

Just as my students stood to say the prayer, my classroom door opened without the courtesy of a knock, and into my classroom walked a casual relief teacher whom I recognized.

The young man walked up to my desk and informed me that he was here to replace me, as I was wanted in the Principal's office for a meeting.

I looked at him very closely and saw the hint of a snigger play around the corners of his lips, so drawing myself up to my full height of 5ft 2ins, I said to him in a firm, but controlled voice, "I am not going anywhere " and with that, I turned to my class who were eagerly watching us both, as they could sense that something was afoot, and I began to say our usual prayer and the class then automatically joined in and the young man had no choice but to vacate my classroom.

Later, when I returned to the staffroom, another note was on my desk informing me that the Union Representative had cancelled the meeting.

After this blatant abuse of power and miscommunication by the Principal, I was informed by the Union that I would now have an interview with the Head of the Union and I felt hopeful that justice was near at hand.

The night before I had my appointment, I had a dream showing me a man, whose legs were missing from the knees down, so I knew that it meant that this particular representative had no legs to stand on and so was not going to be able to help me.

In fact, at our meeting, his behavior had been pretty objectionable because of his cavalier and dismissive manner towards my complaints of being denied opportunities to teach the subjects that I had been employed to teach, as well as the lack of employment opportunities and professional development afforded to me.

He informed me in an arrogant tone of voice that he did not usually deal with people like me but he had heard so much about me that he wanted to meet me himself.

His tone was condescending and belittling and he was decidedly unsupportive and the second time that I met with him, he casually and without batting an eyelid, handed me a copy of a fax he had received from the Independent School that instructed him to inform me, that my teaching position had been suspended and that I was not to return to school.

I also discovered later, from papers that I subpoenaed, that if I did return to school, the police would be contacted and that I would be taken to the Psychiatric Unit at the local hospital for evaluation.

This was because I had returned to school to collect my personal belongings that I had been unable to get previously, because of the underhanded way in which I had been notified of my suspension. However, the obvious delight of the students to see me back at school and their natural inquisitiveness about my sudden disappearance became another problem for the Principal.

To prevent the possibility of it happening again, the Principal contacted the local Police station and claimed that I had frightened both staff and students and that should I return to school again, requested that the police apprehend me and take me to the Hospital for a psychological evaluation.

The fact that a wife of one of the local police worked at the school in no small way contributed to the failure of the Police to be impartial.

The local police were not so quick to act a few years previously, when the school was under another Principal, and a male teacher was transferred to the school to avoid detection from investigating Police for suspected paedophile behaviour, a fact that staff were aware of, but justice did finally catch up with this particular individual and he later died in jail.

Now suddenly, just like that and without a note of regret, a virtual stranger informed me that despite twenty years of employment, I was suspended but the implication was suspension with a view to termination.

I still believe that the course of action taken here by the Independent School was illegal, as there had been a blatant lack of procedural fairness and I was not informed in person about the suspension, but through a third party.

The union representative was instructed to give me this information from a fax that he had received just before my visit.

The fact that even he did not question this course of action, or appear to think it unusual, only served to convince me of the collusion between the Independent school and the Union and my dream of the man who was unable to stand on his own two feet, emphasized how impotent the Union was in its dealings with the powerful Independent School Board.

Also, the fact that the union representative arranged for me to have an interview with a union lawyer, who then tried to manipulate me into making admissions that were taken out of context and that the doctored content of this interview was later given to the legal representative of the Independent school, to be used as a weapon against me in the Industrial Relations Commission, not only breaches client attorney privilege, but flies in the face of what the Union is supposed to stand for.

Fortunately, at the Industrial Relations Commission I was able to retain my composure as the frustrated lawyer for the Independent school harassed and badgered me while I was in the witness box, demanding that I agree that I had made certain admissions to the union lawyer that were contained in the letter that he brandished like some kind of trophy, in front of my face.

I simply asked if my signature was on the document that he held before me.

My composure was the result of a dream that I had dreamed the previous night, about a well dressed man looking through a garbage bin and finding nothing.

The man had three menacing black dogs on a chain and despite pulling a gate in front of me, one of the dogs thrust its head at me, between one of the bars, but when I drew the man's attention to the dog's behaviour, he pulled the dog back into line.

In the dream there was also a huge wind tugging at everyone as they tried to keep their balance, but a thickset man stood behind me, protecting me and preventing me from being swept away.

I could see a flash of something white and a voice said, 'The world will remember this day!'

The well dressed man obviously represented the Commissioner, the menacing black dogs, the lawyer for the Independent school and the man protecting me, was my older son who had come with me to the Industrial Relations Commission to lend support.

The fact that in my dream, there was nothing in the garbage bin, reassured me that there was nothing that could be used against me.

The world represents the experience of what happened and I was shown that it would not be forgotten and later I had a little dragon tattooed on my back as a reminder of the event.

The strong wind represents a principal we feel passionately about and can also be a warning of danger to our security. A wind in a dream can also represent Spirit, as in help from those who have passed over, or it can represent the Holy Spirit inspiring us with wisdom and knowledge.

In the Industrial Relations Commission, the frustrated lawyer was quite obnoxious in his behaviour, and like a cat playing with a trapped mouse, he demanded that I stand up one minute and then sit down the next, and realising that he was not going to achieve his desired coup, the Industrial Relations Commissioner told him in an exasperated fashion, to move on to the next point in his argument.

The lawyer's behaviour gives credence to Geoffrey Robertson's assertion that a lawyer is like a taxi driver and will take anyone's fare, insinuating a lack of scruples on the part of lawyers. The intimidating and bullying behaviour demonstrated here was a testimony to this assertion.

Meanwhile, my older son had been sitting in his seat, 'goggle eyed' at the exhibition he had just witnessed and later on we were both able to relish the little, though short lived victory, that I had won that day, but there were other days that were not so victorious.

At the Industrial Relations Commission, the lawyer for the Independent school had managed to coerce me, into reluctantly signing a Contract, that I would accept a paltry sum of money, which they claimed was compensation for my situation, but that I had insisted was in lieu of lost wages, as I was still legally employed, even though I had been suspended without pay, and I had tenure of employment, a fact that was consistently ignored throughout the proceedings.

A point that was ratified by the representative of the Independent School when he told the Commissioner, that I would be reinstated at my school, on condition that I tendered my resignation immediately.

However one coup that I managed to achieve was in preventing the Independent school from having the term, "Without Prejudice" included in the Contract.

This was extremely important as the term is the opposite of what it implies.

When it is included in a contract it means that a concession made in the course of settlement negotiations or even a fact that an offer of comprise was made, cannot be disclosed, if made on a "Without prejudice" basis.

This tactic prevents the injured party from disclosing what really happened and so enables organizations to continue their nefarious practices.

I could not help but feel a sense of 'Institutional Collusion' in the Industrial Relations Commission when the Commissioner insisted, despite my written objections, that a reference that was detrimental to my future employment opportunities be included in the terms of settlement.

The fact that the Contract was null and void because of the failure of the Independent School to adhere to the time stated on the agreement for payment of the money, was consistently ignored by everyone but me, and only served to further illustrate, what an ass the Independent school was making of the law, with its blatant contempt for due legal process.

Instead of paying the money as agreed on the signed contract, by the close of business on a specified day, the Independent School arrogantly thumbed its nose at the legal document and failed to pay by the due date and it was not until threats were made to have the case relisted, that payment was made two weeks later. The delay in time incurred an increased tax on the sum of money, as it was the beginning of a new tax year, another ploy no doubt, to further financially cripple me. Also, the money received, was little over half of the agreed sum.

That a 'Deed Of Release,' (a document that terminates the litigation in question) was filed in June without my knowledge and consent, before the requirements of the Contract had been fulfilled, beggar's belief and indicates not incompetence, but skulduggery.

After this debacle, the pitiful amount I received did not even cover my lost wages and the Independent school laughed all the way to the bank.

Sadly the firm who represented me in Court was no match for the heavy handed tactics of the Independent School Board and allowed themselves to be manipulated into deceitfully and not to mention illegally, filing the 'Deed of Release 'on my behalf, before payment of the money was received, a crucial part of the Contract.

I only discovered this perfidy when I tried later to have my case relisted at the Industrial Relations Commission.

Also, the documents tendered to the Industrial Relations Commission were doctored, so that misinformation regarding my claim for reinstatement was deleted on the document given to the lawyer representing the Independent school, but not on the Commissioner's document and not on mine.

This deliberate oversight caused misunderstandings and unnecessary aggression from Independent school's representative, as he was unaware of all the facts of the case and simply believed that I was only interested in getting as much money as I could in compensation and he was completely unaware that I was really only interested in returning to my teaching position, but without the harassment.

However, getting back to my meeting with the union representative and the part he played in helping to minimise the fallout from the situation, on behalf of the Independent school, to prevent staff from being aware of what was really going on.

This is another ploy that organizations resort to, in their efforts to silence a whistle blower, or reformer.

The organization goes into damage control if their attempts to silence the individual have been unsuccessful and in order to minimize the damage and prevent any sympathetic support from others as well as preventing the individual being attributed the status of Martyr, the organization encourages others to respond to the whistle blower as a sick or greedy individual.

The Head of the Union had tried to brow beat me into giving up my fight for justice, claiming that he thought I had psychological problems and was imagining things.

This smacked of similar accusations levelled at The Magdalene Girls in Ireland, who had been sent to Convents for unmarried mothers, by their parents, who had been ashamed of them for getting pregnant out of wedlock and who were sexually abused by priests, while in the care of the nuns.

When these tragic girls tried to report the abuse, they were locked up in Mental Institutions as the belief was; they had to be mad to say what they said about the priests.

Sadly this shameful behaviour by the Irish nuns and priests continued into the mid nineties and the consequence of this conspiracy of silence still remains within these institutions.

An aunt of mine who is now deceased and who gave testimony in Court against a priest in the late nineties about the sexual abuse that he perpetrated against children in her care, sent me a letter of support in my fight for justice, a copy of which I later submitted to the Federal Magistrate's Court to substantiate my case about manipulation of evidence.

Chapter Seven

Fait Accompli

On the day that I was seeing the Union Representative and being told that I was suspended, the staff at my school was being told that I would not be back to school that year and that a casual teacher had already been employed to cover my classes, so confident was the Independent school about the complicity of the President of the Union, that wheels for a replacement were already set in motion, before I even knew about the suspension.

It was at this stage that I had a dream telling me that a little girl had been murdered and everyone knew about it and nobody said anything.

To dream of a murder indicates a violent end to a situation, usually in an emotional or psychological manner and a little girl suggests the innocence of the victim.

I knew then that I would not be allowed to return to my school.

When the local police, with the assistance of a psychiatrist, tried later to have me detained under the mental health act, I decided to subpoena papers from both the Police and the Mental Health facility and it was then that I discovered the huge lengths that the Principal of the school had gone to, in her attempt to silence me.

Because I had failed to be reinstated in my school at the Industrial Relations Commission, I decided to continue my fight to disprove the falsehoods spread by the Principal of the Independent school and so I contacted the Industrial Relations Commission a few months later, with the intention of continuing my fight for reinstatement to my teaching position.

I also applied to teach in the State Education system and I was given an interview at which I was informed that I would be recommended as,' suitable for employment.'

Ironically, it was only twenty days after this successful interview, that my close family member whom I had not seen in four or five years, contacted the Division of Mental Health and based on the information supplied to her, claimed that I was paranoid, socially phobic, as well as delusional and had been fired from school two years previously, due to stalking a staff member, but believed that it was the other way round.

The timing of this tissue of lies was dumbfounding!

I had just three months previously been in the Industrial Relations Commission with the Independent school, and had recently been recommended as suitable for employment in the State school system and here was my close family member, coming out with ridiculous claims regarding my employment status and emotional and mental health, based on a pretext of concern for my well being.

This close family member also stated that the school had offered to pay for a psychological examination with a particular psychiatrist, but that I had claimed that the psychiatrist had refused to do the assessment.

A psychological assessment is a strategy used by quite a number of various Independent and Private schools, who insist on paying for the assessment, so that the information gleaned can be manipulated against the individual and used to the organization's advantage.

The last statement by the close family member is true and unfortunately there is always an element of truth wrapped up in any fabrication, which gives credence to the other falsehoods. I did agree to have a psychological examination as required by the Independent school, as I was told that my position would be terminated if I refused to follow what they referred to as, a lawful and reasonable request. However the nominated psychiatrist declined to do the assessment, citing a conflict of personal interests, and so I went to a different psychiatrist who was recommended by my doctor, who was overseeing my workers' compensation claim for anxiety and stress, due to being bullied in the work place.

A Workers Compensation Case, I might add, that had been acknowledged by the Independent school, in its 'Notification of Injury/ Claim for Workers' Compensation' and signed by the Worker Compensation Claim Officer, after they received a Work Cover Medical Certificate from my doctor, before any litigation ever took place.

The psychiatrist that I did see was based at a Specialist Medical Centre and he provided me with a medical certificate that was dated and signed, to give to the Principal of my school stating that 'There is no psychological or psychiatric reason which would prevent this woman from returning to full gainful employment.'

The Principal deliberately withheld this information from the Representative of the Independent School Board, who harassed and bullied me even more, believing that I was being deliberately uncooperative, and it was only at the Industrial Relations Commission when truth came out about the psychological assessment and the representative said in a surprised voice 'I didn't know,' that we both fully comprehended, the vile nature of the Principal and the Independent School Board.

The fact that I was sacked on the basis of the lie that I had refused to have a psychological assessment, seemed to have escaped everyone's notice and instead of reinstatement as justice demanded, the tide of events simply swept along the course that the Principal and the Independent School Board had intended.

It is interesting to note here that neither the female teacher's aide, nor the other teacher involved, were ever required to have a psychological assessment, nor were they required to take leave while the situation was under investigation.

Now, once again the Principal was deliberately withholding the truth to further her own ends.

Attempts to prevent me from having my case reopened and to prevent employment opportunities, were behind the latest move to have me placed in a Mental Health Facility.

Because of financial hardship, the unusual delay in having my teaching qualifications processed, also caused further anxiety and eventually I went to my local Member of Parliament and successfully canvassed his help in securing employment within the State Education system.

It was the following February however, that the psychiatrist and the accompanying police officer came to my door, despite submissions about her supposed concern, having been made by my close family member six months previously.

When I went to the local Court and requested a subpoena to be served at both the Mental Health Unit and the local Police station to find out what was going on, I was only then made aware of the time difference between the two incidences and the information provided on the papers that were subpoenaed, indicated that I had been continually under surveillance, and everything I did and everywhere I went, was recorded from the time when my family member contacted the Mental Health Unit, to the day six months later when the police and psychiatrist arrived at my door.

This revelation explained the several bizarre incidents that happened over the previous months, where complete strangers would suddenly approach me and make unusual comments about items of clothing I was wearing, or canvass my opinion in unexpected places, such as the time when I came through an exit barrier at the train station and was approached by a young woman who wanted to know what I thought about the Irish.

Another time a lady surprised me by crossing over the street to tell me how much she admired my dress and yet another lady did a similar thing to admire my handbag.

And another incident happened on the local train, where a

lady sat down beside me, despite other unoccupied seats being available, and proceeded to open her newspaper and spread the pages to their full width, right in front of my face. As she perused the newspaper, seemingly oblivious to my obvious discomfort at having the newspaper thrust so close to my face, as well as blocking my view, I felt compelled to point out that she would have more room in the unoccupied seat in front.

With a blistering look of contempt in my direction, the lady folded her newspaper and moved to the other seat.

That I refused to open my door to the police and psychiatrist is a point of law.

Once a door has been opened on a voluntary basis, there is a presumption that access has been granted to the police and then there is little you can do to stop them apprehending you, or prevent other activities that might involve questionable behaviour.

By refusing to open the door, whatever plans were afoot to haul me off to the Mental Health Unit, were scuttled by my lack of cooperation.

The next day I presented myself at the local Police station to reassure the Police visitor from the previous day that his concerns for me were totally unfounded.

Ironically, what was happening around me, finally explained the meaning of a dream that I had the previous year.

In my dream, I saw students in my year eleven class, sitting in their usual row of seats when suddenly; my eyes fell on one, dark haired student of South American background, who was quietly working away.

Someone in the dream then said, "He has been chosen for the higher learning, as he is the best in his class."

This dream surprised me, as this particular student did not appear to be outstanding in anyway, in fact if anything, was quite shy and self effacing.

The higher learning I now realised was the awareness of the far reaching tentacles of the Independent school and the lengths that it will go to, in order to silence its detractors.

The student obviously represented me, and I realised that my Northern Ireland background of growing up in "The Troubles" had prepared me well for what was happening and this was why I was, according to my dream, "the best in my class".

Other teachers in the school, who had been harassed and bullied, had allowed themselves to be moved on to different schools outside the area, after signing documents that guaranteed their silence, a ploy that the Independent school tried to use unsuccessfully with me in the Industrial Relations Commission.

The people of South America, like the Irish, have deep spiritual roots, which tie them to the land and like the Irish, the coming of Christianity replaced their deep, rich cultural belief system, with a superstitious belief in a Christ as a Redeemer, which not even the hierarchy of the Catholic Church believe in.

Pope Leo X is reported to have said, "It has served us well, this myth of Christ".

The essential belief of Transubstantiation that forms the centre of the Catholic faith earns the Protestant clergy's contemptuous term "Hocus- Pocus" and is a distortion of the Latin words, Hoc Est Enim Corpus Meum "This is My Body" and is generally directed against magical practices of both the Catholic Priest and the magician.

W.B. Yeats, the most distinguished of Irish poets and playwrights in the twentieth century, wrote that the 'Second Coming' will not be Christ as Christians believe, but Paganism, because of the disillusionment and suppression suffered under Christianity.

Nostradamus also spoke of the end of the papacy because of its corruption and the time that he prophesied is nearer than many people realize.

The failure of other staff members who had also experienced bullying and harassment, but who did not have the stamina to stand up against the injustice of their particular situations, was due in no small measure to their backgrounds, which had not prepared them to fight.

Growing up in Northern Ireland, I was constantly reminded of my obligation to stand up for my beliefs and to be prepared to die for my religion. This was drummed into me from my early years in primary school, to my final years in high school.

Indeed my Northern Irish background, has served me well.

The acute disappointment and disillusionment of my experiences was quickly replaced with a reality check about my situation, when I had a dream asking, "Who else but you, Brave Heart?"

I felt like Adam and Eve in the Garden of Eden, I had lost my sense of innocence and I would never be the same again.

The seeds of courage under fire were sown in my subconscious mind from the beginning.

It was now time to stop feeling sorry for myself and once again, play the hand that I had been dealt.

Born under the astrological sign of Mars, the Roman God of War, like all Aries individuals, when faced with thorny paths and situations of conflict, because of a moral conviction, I have the courage and strength to go the distance.

It is of interest to note here, that my Astrological sign of Aries was also shared by the now deceased family member, who stood up in Court, against the sexual abuse of children in her care.

The line of Mars that runs down the inside of my life line on both hands, is a testimony to that courage and one that Roman Generals of old used to look for, in the hands of soldiers going into battle. This line indicates that the individual is not afraid to die in battle. Indeed my father often used to warn me that I could not take on the whole world, when I complained about the inequalities and injustices of the Northern Ireland situation.

Chapter Eight

Family Matters

It is sad and disappointing when family members choose to side with those in power against one of their own, but if you dig deeply enough, you will find the reason why.

My distant family relative, who had taught with me for so many years prior to changing to a school nearer home, held a bitter resentment towards my family because of assistance rendered to her family, by my father after the premature death of her own father.

This bitterness only came to light in a drunken surge of emotion many years previously and took me quite by surprise. I had no idea that she resented my family's help, so much.

She was only too aware of the machinations of the Independent School system and its expectations of middle management in its schools, as having once given up her role as co-ordinator, because of the increasing size of her young family; she confided in me that she was appalled when the then Principal, called her a traitor for resigning her post.

Obviously her knowledge of the inner workings of middle management was a problem and by labelling her a traitor, the Principal was making her aware of obligations to the same and so ensuring her silence.

With the changeover of Principal, her services were once again called into action.

I was surprised to see her turn up at the school staffroom one day, while I was having lunch.

She did not acknowledge me, but sat with her back to me, while she chatted to one of the co-ordinators. When the co-ordinator left the staffroom, she remained seated with her back to me.

I realized then, that the Principal had enlisted her help but I was blissfully unaware at the time, in what kind of nefarious fashion.

As for other family members, my relationship with them suffered from the religious bigotry so common amongst the Irish and which superseded any prior family concerns.

My divorce caused estrangement from my immediate family, as my mother now preferred only "paying members" according to my dream, in other words family members whom my mother could be proud of, instead of those who were an embarrassment, whether from divorce or other behaviour.

If only my mother had listened to the wise advice given by Irish playwright Oscar *Wilde*;

"There is only one thing in this world worse than be talked about and that is, not being talked about."

I was given this information in a dream after discovering by accident, that one of my brothers was getting married and that I had not been invited to the wedding, as my mother did not want the bride's father, a fellow Irishman, to know that I was divorced.

It is hardly surprising therefore, that my family did actively try to undermine my case against this Independent school with the full blessing of my mother.

As for my close family member, according to my dreams, she capitalized on the situation to make herself look good at my expense. She had been the cleverest of us all but she had failed to achieve the academic success that she was capable of until almost middle aged and so had spent years in the back ground, watching others take the stage and bathe in the limelight, while she sat in the wings, waiting for her chance to shine.

Perhaps it was because of her wilfulness as a child that she chose not to apply herself in her early years at school, or she may have just been thumbing her nose at the control exercised by establishment, being clever enough to see through its ploys and illusions.

Family rivalry and vanity no doubt were at the root of her behaviour.

As frightening as the attempt to have me committed had been, other just as frightening events, also took place.

Personal blood samples were sent to an unauthorized doctor in a pharmaceutical laboratory, with no satisfactory explanation given.

A few months later however, I suffered a severe chronic reaction to a new drug prescribed to me by a visiting doctor, that replaced the standard medication that I had been described by my regular doctor, for a chronic illness that I suffered from.

I was unable to contact this doctor when I had the severe reaction and I never saw him again.

At different times, I was run off the road in my car, had my car egged, tyres slashed, headlights kicked in, and eventually had my car written off completely by my insurer, because of the amount of vandalism that my car had been subjected to.

At first, I had thought that a person in the block of flats where I resided was to blame for the slashed tyres and my car being egged, because of her unwarranted verbal abuse and vulgar behaviour of dropping her trousers and baring her bare bum in my direction, colloquially known as "chucking brown eyes" because of a dispute regarding external doors being left open at night that enabled feral cats and other animals to enter the building and defecate on the floors leaving a perpetual smell of urine in the hallway.

I applied to the local Court for an A.V.O. against her initially and then on the advice from my dreams, decided instead to request mediation, after a fiasco at the Court on the day of the Hearing, and try to resolve the situation as amicably as possible.

My dream had also warned me against the overuse of Court resources, as I had already tried to take an A.V.O. out previously, to stop my family from interfering in my pursuit of justice.

I did not manage to get an A.V.O. against my family, as I refused to take the stand after also being warned against it in a dream. I was shown that a family member was trying to invoke a little known and infrequently used, old fashioned Law, called the Law of Domicile.

This law enables a family member who is a native of a British Colony, to assume control over another family member, if they are concerned for the health of the person, or if it can be proven that the person is incapacitated in some way.

In the dream I found myself to be a prisoner in the Stocks. I had my head and hands pushed through and restricted by the small opening in the Stocks, an antiquated form of punishment used in centuries gone by, in the British Isles.

The dream at first perplexed me, but the following day when I was at the local markets, I picked up a second hand Law Book to browse through and the first page I opened at random in the book, explained the Law of Domicile.

It is said that there are no coincidences in life and the serendipity of happenings in my search for justice leads to believe that this is true.

I was horrified to see what my dream alluded to and what my family member was up to.

When I went to Court with my family member, I noticed that we were ushered into a private room away from the main area and for some unknown reason; I was surprised to see a video player or projector in the room.

When my family member came into the room after me, with a professional looking individual in tow, who took a seat some yards behind her, I immediately became suspicious of what was going on as no explanation was given for his presence and he was not introduced to me.

When my family member stood up to speak, she used legal

jargon and cited legal codes of law that meant nothing to me and the terms were not explained to me.

No doubt she had been briefed to do this, so that I would be unaware of what was afoot.

My sons were called in turn, to give evidence on my behalf, and then after they had given enough evidence to disprove the falsehoods that my family member had written to the Mental Health Unit, I was asked to take the stand.

Upon declining to do so, the Judge informed me that by not doing so, he would be unable to grant my A.V.O. But still I refused to do so, as my dream had warned me not to take the stand.

The Judge then seemed to have a dilemma, as if he was not prepared for this unexpected turn of events; after all I had made application for the A.V.O.

After a moment of heavy silence, the Judge said that he would take a short break to consider a judgement on the case and he left the Court Room.

When he returned shortly afterwards, the Judge said that he would make a ruling on the matter and he ruled that it would be put on record, that I was a good mother and a good teacher.

And that was good enough for me.

I may not have gotten my A.V.O. but it was now set in concrete as my dream had shown me that I was a good mother and a good teacher and no lies could change that.

The night before the court case, I had a dream where I saw the Madonna and child carved out of a large rock, so I knew that I was protected and now it was carved in stone that I was a good mother.

Now we will return to the mediation session regarding the vandalism of my car. Both the Mediator and I were astonished to discover that the police had told the person that I was in litigation with that I was a Mental Case and to ignore everything I said.

The Court fiasco on the day of the original hearing was the result of advice given to this individual, to take an A.V.O. out against me, on the day set down for the original Hearing.

My case had been postponed on the day of the hearing, while I was in the Court, because according to the sitting Judge, the defendant was too ill to attend Court.

In fact the defendant was already in an office in the Court House, with a Registrar and applying for an A.V.O. against me, at that precise time and with the collusion of Court officials, who falsified information on the application form to disguise what, was really going on, a copy of which I still have in my possession.

The person's disrespectful behaviour was obviously influenced by what the police had told her.

Chapter Nine

Pretty Woman
in Reverse

After this, I discovered that I had become unemployable, or if I managed to get casual work, there always seemed to be a problem.

Eventually I was reduced to getting food vouchers from a Welfare Agency, as opportunities for any kind of work dried up completely, as did my ability to pay my rent.

Unlike Julia Roberts in *Pretty Woman*, who went from economic hardship to wealth, I experienced the reverse, going from a privileged upbringing to the fringes of society.

My circumstances reached rock bottom and the only room I could afford to rent, turned out to be in a house owned by a drug dealer and his ice-addicted girlfriend.

This final humiliating step was the end result of harassment and bullying at other rental properties that I had lived at and in the space of five years, I had to move seven times.

The owner of this particular establishment was a slightly built, weedy kind of bloke, with sores erupting all over his face and shifty brown eyes that flickered around the room as he spoke.

His girlfriend was a tall, dark haired and olive skinned beauty, whose mother had come from an exotic location and her father was an Australian missionary priest, who had left the priesthood after meeting and falling in love with her mother.

Her childhood it seemed, had been one of defiance towards her father's overly strict and controlling paranoid behaviour, which was a consequence of his self inflicted sense of guilt, from leaving the Church.

In the house there were no locks on any of the internal doors, not even the bathroom, or the toilet, the most private room of the house. Only on the front and back door were bolted locks of a forbidding nature.

The lack of blinds on my bedroom windows and the draughty bare floor boards that allowed the wind to creep through and who knows what else, caused me grave concern, until I covered the floor with a ragged mat that I bought at an op shop and pinned a spare sheet across the window.

Too late, I realised how precarious my predicament had become.

Initially, the couple seemed to be friendly and hospitable, but then I began to notice that things began to go missing from the boxes in my unlocked bedroom and my food began disappearing from the fridge.

I tried to ignore these little incidents however, as I was grateful for somewhere to stay.

Even when the male had to attend Court on what he said were false drug charges, I went to Court with him and his girlfriend to lend support.

How unbelievably naive of me!

I began to notice that when the couple quarrelled and the female would become shrill and accusatory, the male would suggest that they go out for a walk.

When they returned from their walk, I always noticed that there would be a strange detachment about the female, and she would turn the music up loud and hum to herself as she did her household chores. The male of course, would be gone by this time having sudden urgent business that needed attending to.

I realised that the walk suggested by the male, was as a ploy to lure the female away from the house to supply her with something to calm her down.

I also noticed other people turn up at the front door of the house and after a short negotiation; an exchange of some sort would take place.

Things began to turn sour when the house owner confided in me that he liked me and was intending to take his partner to visit her family in outback Australia, and dump her there.

He told me that he had met his partner at a wife swapping party that he and his former wife had attended, after seeing it advertised in the local paper.

The couples had hit it off so well, that his wife had gone off permanently with the other man and the other man's partner had stayed with him, but now he wanted rid of her.

I was horrified and I decided to warn the girl of his intentions as I thought, 'What a lousy thing to do!' And besides, I certainly didn't want his attentions.

That was a big mistake! He denied everything and claimed that I was making it up and she chose to believe him. After all he was her drug supplier!

I was terrorised at night by the couple. The electricity was switched off and several times the male owner tried to gain access to my room when he thought I was asleep, but I had barricaded the door with the few pieces of furniture, that I had managed to bring with me and that served as a slight deterrent.

When the owner had slyly tried to open my bedroom door and met with unexpected resistance, he became vicious and angry and he and his girlfriend would hurl verbal, racist abuse at me, through the bedroom door.

The owner's girlfriend who turned out to be a prostitute and plied her trade at a local brothel, began to walk around the house naked during the day and drape herself over her boyfriend's legs, in lewd and offense poses to deliberately cause embarrassment and to make me feel as uncomfortable as possible, so that I would leave.

But leaving was impossible for me. The only money I possessed was from Centre link and I had no way of getting a bond together, also I had nowhere to go.

The terror I began to experience over the next few weeks was indescribable.

Chapter Ten

The Terrorist at the Bed Room Door

When I had grown up in Northern Ireland during *The Troubles,* there was a lot of frightening terrorist activity by various hard line groups, but this terror was completely different.

In Northern Ireland, everyone was terrorised in one form or another, but at least a little comfort could be drawn from the fact that it was a shared experience, here I was on my own and no one knew what was happening to me.

At night I would keep a candle lit, because the electricity had been turned off and I would try to stay awake, to make sure nothing happened to me while I was asleep.

One night in particular I was so tired that I dozed off but suddenly woke up startled from a dream where a voice was urging me to wake up immediately, as my father was here.

I woke up to find that the candle wick had burned down till it was dangerously close to my hair.

Another minute or so, and I would have been set on fire.

My father, who is dead, had obviously been watching over me and alerted me in my dream, to the imminent danger.

Shortly after this I met my partner and at first the owner of the house abused him and warned him off his property, when he came to visit me.

However, being a builder by profession, my partner knew that he had legal right of access to the front door and said as much.

Then fearing for my safety, my two sons' accessed money from their savings, which their grandfather had bequeathed to them, and they lent it to me, to help me pay for a bond and they also went flat hunting with me as I now wanted to find a flat which was as far away as possible from the living nightmare of my current accommodation.

Once suitable accommodation had been found, my partner and my older son helped me to move.

The owner was livid that I was moving out and denigrated my character to my older son, as he helped me to pack up my belongings.

I had come to realize that this man was very dangerous and perhaps even slightly unhinged from years of drug abuse.

He followed my son and me up and down the pathway, yelling vile torrents of abuse at us, as we slowly and carefully moved my remaining possessions up to the waiting car and we tried not to exacerbate the situation any further, by responding to his malicious and spiteful taunting.

CHAPTER ELEVEN

DUE PROCESS

When family members turned a blind eye to the truth and tried unsuccessfully to have me sectioned under the mental health act, the local police took it upon themselves to illegally put me on their data system as a person under the mental health act, so that when I made a complaint about what was happening I was not taken seriously, either by the police, or by the judiciary.

On one occasion when I went to the local Police Station to make a complaint, a female officer who had been standing on the other side of the counter, looked at me as I came through the front door and then seemed to glance at something above her head and in one instant, her demeanour towards me changed and she became quite hostile and then a really bizarre thing happened.

When I said that I would like to make a complaint about an incident of harassment, the female police officer stepped back away from the counter and then began to march up and down the room and shouted in a belligerent tone of voice, "we don't have to listen to you; we don't have to help you," and continued to repeat this mantra, as if it had been a set of instructions that needed to be remembered.

In fact her behaviour was so strange that a young male officer who was standing in the background observing this strange exhibition and who obviously felt uncomfortable by police woman's behaviour came over to me and said that he would take my statement.

Later on I did bring this matter to the attention of a sitting Judge, as it was important for me to keep an official Police record of the myriad of seemingly unconnected little incidents that besieged me, which individually may have seemed trivial, but when put together in the context of a deliberate harassment campaign, appeared in a completely different light.

It was on the advice of a Judge from the District Court that I had gone to the Police Station in the first place, as he advised me to have a proper police record of facts, to substantiate my case.

Another even more bizarre incident happened not long after this.

As I was driving to one of my dancing lessons, which were being held at a local pub, memories from my student days in Manchester for some unknown reason, came flooding into my mind.

I had attended an all female, teacher training College and I was reliving fond memories of how we would all sing on the bus that collected us from College and shepherded us to and fro from the many dancing parties that we attended en masse.

The Irish were heavily represented at the College and rarely if ever, missed getting on the bus and heading out for a good night's 'craic' and we sang everywhere we went.

I am not lucky enough to possess a fine singing voice like so many of my fellow countrymen, but still I also like to sing.

And so, as I drove along the quiet streets towards my dancing-class venue, I began to sing a favourite Irish song, known as *The Butcher Boy*.

Upon reaching the designated venue, I parked my car and entered the premises.

As I walked through the front door fear gripped my heart as I saw flashing on and off on the overhead screen the words *The Butcher Boy, The Butcher Boy, The Butcher Boy, The Butcher Boy, The Butcher Boy.*

Despite being somewhat shaken by this sight, I decided that I was not going to let whoever was behind it win and stayed for my dancing class, as if nothing untoward had happened.

Ironically, for the first time ever, that evening I was stopped and breathalysed by the local Police on my way home.

It would appear that a type of corporate conspiracy operates within the court system, in favour of the employer and especially in relation to the Board of the Independent School system.

As *Geoffrey Robertson* illustrates in his book, justice is just a game and only those in power will win. No matter how honourable or deserving an applicant may be, unless they have power, money, or celebrity status, the Court will rarely look upon them with favour. The ordinary person in the street is simply there to keep the wheels of law in motion and they only serve as a mere pawn in the charade called justice that allows those on stage to strut their stuff.

I was reminded of a line from a poem by *Charles Causley* that states," The Law is as tricky as a ten foot snake."

Even when I wrote a letter of complaint to the Police Commissioner about the behaviour of the police, my complaint was dismissed as too trivial to warrant attention.

At the Industrial Relations Commission, despite falsified documents being filed without my consent, that terminated my appeal against my unfair and unlawful dismissal, permission was denied to have my case reopened, despite presenting a letter of permission to do so, by the then Minister of Industrial Relations.

At a meeting with a member of the Human Rights and Equal Opportunities Commission, my case was trivialised by their representative and dismissed as unimportant.

On the way home, I was shoulder charged from behind, as I walked along the street and my son who was with me at the time, witnessed the strange behaviour of a man who appeared to be following us through the underground station and who seemed to be quite taken aback, when we turned around unexpectedly to go in a different direction and nearly bumped into him, so closely was he trailing us from behind.

False information was submitted by my employer to The Administrative Decisions Tribunal, regarding their grounds for dismissal and several staff members were coerced into making false statements. Also the details of the two staff members involved were incorrectly recorded as two teachers, instead of a teacher's aide and a teacher. I believe that this mistake was deliberate as it would have raised eyebrow at the Administrative Decisions Tribunal, that a teacher's aide was being legally represented by the Independent school, against a teacher with a spotless track record.

A dream that I had about little houses being tacked on, one on top of another in a precarious fashion and in imminent danger of collapsing, informed me of how the Independent school, was manipulating staff, as each house represented another person that had been add to the fictitious list of accusations.

A further dream of watching a group of people shackled together and being herded into what seemed to be a windowless van, also made me aware of the difficult position other staff members of the school had been placed in if they wanted to keep their jobs.

I believe a fear of reprisal from the Hierarchy, or wanting to be on the winning side, may have been behind the acquiescence of some staff members to this subterfuge.

A multitude of little things designed to annoy and frustrate me in my search for justice, hounded me every step of the way.

Fortunately, my dreams alerted me to the evil machinations of both ambitious family members and the Principal of the Independent school and helped me to outwit my detractors, as well as enabling me to pursue my fight for justice single-handed, through the tricky corridors of the Australian Court System.

My dreams encouraged me to fight for my rights by reassuring me that it did not matter if I were to win or lose, it was only important to get the truth out there.

And so, armed only whatever information came to me in my dreams, I managed to leave a paper trail through the court system of Australia that should anyone ever care to take a look, will demonstrate the great lengths that those with power will go to, in order to destroy the life and career of any individual who has the temerity to question its behaviour.

The Ten Commandments of the Old Testament which have also been usurped by Christianity are meaningless to those in power.

They simply serve as a yoke to burden the common man, to keep him in his place and stop him from questioning the pretenders to Spiritual knowledge and the Law.

Developing an internal locus of control is essential, for anyone who wishes to be free and no longer be a slave to Men who masquerade under a cloak of Christianity and who wield inordinate amounts of power that cripples the soul of the individual.

I have a tremendous faith in a Higher Power and my Celtic belief in reincarnation encourages me to continue to do checks and balances in every aspect of my life, as I do not intend to continue these lessons in my next reincarnation.

It is for this reason that I renounced under oath, my Irish religious belief system.

Prior to renouncing my Irish religious heritage, I had a dream that I was climbing a mountain. As I was climbing to the top of the mountain, the path wound its way round and round the mountain, in an ever upward direction. Eventually I reached the summit of the mountain which overlooked the ocean and taking a leap of faith, I dived off the mountain top and into the ocean and the frothy wake of a boat that had just passed by and around me I could hear people crying.

When we climb a mountain in our dreams, we are making the effort necessary for progress in our lives.

Climbing a mountain also represents the ability to access the grandeur within and to be the best that you can possibly be.

The mountain reminded me of the Island of Maui in Hawaii, which I had once visited with my ex- husband, as a stopover on our way to Ireland to get married and this linked me with the past.

The wake of the boat that I dived into is a play on words, as the

Irish are notorious for their wakes following a death in the family. The fact that I was aware of grief around the wake of the boat which itself represents a relationship, affirmed that the dream was symbolising the death of my belief system and my family attachment to the same.

My battle with the Independent school has left me in an unenviable financial position and my dreams have warned me that despite my ripening years, I will have to continue to earn my own living as fortune has passed me by. A dream I had about a bombed out building, where in the midst of all the rubble, I saw one little red flower growing in a tiny little patch of ground, reassured me that I will overcome my circumstances by harnessing my psychic ability, represented by the little red flower. The dream has also shown me that I will overcome adversity by maintaining a cheerful outlook despite my circumstances and that I will eventually climb through to prominence and happiness.

When I had this dream, I knew that the bombed out building represented me and my life at that point in time, but with determination I, like everyone else, have the ability to rebuild my life.

I do what I have always done, I teach. I teach others how to harness the messages that they receive in their dreams and how to develop their innate intuition and psychic ability, as well as how to meditate.

My dreams have warned me that my fight for justice is not over yet and that there are still problems to be faced in the near future, but as I have said earlier, my Irish upbringing in Northern Ireland, have served me well and no doubt will continue to do so.

The harassment finally stopped when I met my partner, because now I have a witness to what is happening. When two people stand together, they can take on the whole world.

At the beginning of this book, I mentioned the similarities that the Irish have to the Australian Aborigine and now at the conclusion of my story of power and powerlessness, I would like to refer to a renowned aboriginal by the name of Charlie Perkins, who overcame great hardship in his early life, to rise to the status of politician and one who championed the aboriginal cause for equality and justice.

I had a dream in which someone said, 'My name is Perkins. Some say I am from Donegal and some say I am from Dublin' and in the dream the person was telling their story and so I knew that it was now time for me to tell my story.

Donegal is a part of Ireland where one can experience true Irish culture and where in some parts, only the Gaelic language is spoken. The traditional way of life can be experienced firsthand and there is a slower pace to life that allows one to believe in fairies and the Leprechaun with his pot of gold.

Dublin on the other hand is a cosmopolitan hub, teeming with tourists and Grand hotels and Trinity College Dublin with its Book of Kells, which adds a sophisticated cultural edge, that is admired the world over.

My father used to rent a holiday house in both Donegal and Dublin over the years and as children, we enjoyed the contrasting cultural experiences enormously.

The dream suggests the different viewpoints of individuals who will read my story and the contrast in opinions as to why I did what I did.

Some may see me as naive and trusting like the people of Donegal, while others may view me as worldly wise, and knowledgeable and perhaps even an opportunist like the city people of Dublin.

No matter what the opinion of the reader may be, the information given in this book is an accurate description of how those in power and those in an organization will behave, when threatened with a whistle blower, who raises legitimate concerns and it is based on actual facts that can be verified.

Chapter Twelve

Awaken the Dreamer Within

And now it is for you the reader, to use the information included in this book to help you become the best you can possibly be.

The dreaming mind helps us to access the courage we all possess deep within us and this leads on to better health and happier lives.

Throughout this Dream book, I will provide the reader with specific examples of how our dreams enable us to grow as individuals through the type of symbolism that the dreaming mind brings to consciousness.

It is more important for the reader at this stage however, to begin to write down their dreams so that a record can be kept of the progress that the individual is making, as well as alerting them to premonitions.

Also the dreamer will discover that the act of writing down the dream, not only encodes the dream in the memory banks, but it also provides a different perspective on the dream.

I would like to take the opportunity here, to recommend an invaluable technique that I have borrowed from the book, "Rosindubh: The Irish Dream Catcher" by fellow countrywoman,

Rosemary Dawson. This technique enables the dreamer to access answers to specific questions from their dreams.

Before sleep, ask one specific question, e.g. "Is it in my best interests to.....?"

Ask to be given a STATEMENT in your dreams, giving the exact answer to the question.

Ask to remember the STATEMENT.

Then write the STATEMENT down.

It is of great importance that you do this, as laid out for you here, as the technique helps the dreamer to focus on what is important in the dream and not get distracted by the background information or the trimmings so to speak. Only the Statement is important.

In the book, the technique is likened to the Irish Holey Stone.

This is a stone with a hole in the centre and when held up to the eye, allows the individual to focus on their enemies and not get distracted.

The technique can also be compared to shooting an arrow that is guaranteed to hit its mark.

If the answer does not come the first night, repeat the same question.

At the most, it will take three nights to get the answer but for most, the answer will come after one night.

Remember, it does not matter about the context of the dream, only the STATEMENT is important.

To ensure that you remember the information and any premonitions, this Dream Catcher Journal, has been divided into two sections.

At the front there is a section for recording your dreams on a daily basis, as is usual for a Dream Journal, however at the back of this book, there is also a section for the dreamer to note the daily happenings of their waking life, thus ensuring a way for the dreamer to keep a check on the relationship between their dreaming life and their waking life.

In this way, not only will the dreamer understand the general symbolism of dreams but the dreamer will also become aware of how their own personal experiences, affect the type of symbolism that the dreaming mind throws up and of course premonitions can be verified.

The Dream Catcher Journal

Getting Started

An example of the benefits we get from recording both dreams and daily experiences is demonstrated through a dream shared with me by my younger son.

My son rang me on the morning of 19th January one year, to tell me about a dream that he had the night before and which he believed was connected to me.

He said that the dream had informed him that something important was going to happen on August 23rd which I needed to pay attention to.

Often when we dream about our mother, it can refer to the mother within ourselves. My son's dream however, was for me, as the date given was the date of my late father's birthday and as the dead always put an opportunity the way of the living at anniversary times, I knew that something important was coming for me at that time.

As it turned out, I attended a free, Law seminar, dealing with Deceased Estates and Wills on that particular date, which provided me with vital information that I needed regarding a family dispute.

By recording the information that my younger son had given me, the date was firmly etched in my mind and I was able to verify the information later.

This example emphasis how helpful it is to not only record dream information, but by also writing a daily journal of events, we are able to check out, as well as keep track of information received.

In the succeeding pages, an opportunity is provided for the

reader to record their own dreams, with helpful information on particular dream symbolism included at the top of each page.

Other more detailed dream symbolism and examples are also included throughout the book.

Happy Dreaming.

Mother Dreams

The relationship we had with our mothers can influence the type of dream that we have and how we view the different aspects of our personality.

If our relationship with our mother was and still is, a nurturing relationship, then the mother figure in the dream will be likewise.

If however, the relationship was one of criticism and fault finding, then our dream mother may reflect these same characteristics, or the dream may be highlighting the relationship between you and someone who is like your mother.

The person may have the same Astrology sign, or same Chinese year, or the same Numerology number as your mother.

My ex-husband has the same Astrology sign and Numerology number as my mother, leading me to often say in jest,' I married my mother, but I should have married my father'.

The dreaming mind will access whatever information is most suitable to not only draw the dreamer's attention to information needed, but it will also help the dreamer to understand the type of relationship that exists with the individual which their dream is alluding to.

Night time

Night time in a dream indicates there is a time of difficulty around the dreamer and so care needs to be taken in all undertakings. Be aware if time is significant in your dreams, time of day, or time of the year. Nut out any associations you have with the time indicated in the dream.

SChOOL

To dream of a primary school, indicates that you are learning how to meet your basic needs. Dreaming of high school indicates progress in your community and professional life. You are learning about relationships and competitiveness. A University education indicates that the dreamer is now privy to certain information that is not available to everyone. What were your learning experiences at school and what are your dreams drawing your attention to now?

The dream of a particular relationship that we had with others, during a certain school period, is a reflection of the type of relationship now being experienced in a particular circumstance.

Muscles

Muscles in a dream, refer to the emotional and spiritual muscles that we need to develop, to deal with aspects of our nature that are too sensitive, and which hinder us from taking opportunities in our lives.

What is happening in your intimate or professional life that requires a 'workout' at the emotional, mental or spiritual dream gymnasium?

Being Chased

B eing chased in a dream, is alerting us to our fear of taking personal responsibility for our failures, fears and emotions. Who or what is chasing you in your dream? We need to turn and face our fear.

COOKING

C ooking in a dream emphasis the mixing of the ingredients of our lives to be successful, or it can refer to how we nurture others.

PUPPETS

Puppet dreams refer to being manipulated. Who is pulling whose strings?

Ring

A ring in a dream can suggest that a commitment needs to be made to either a person or a situation. It is only when a commitment is made, that we are able to move forward. What is holding you back from making the necessary commitment in your life?

Eye

An awareness of eyes in a dream could be drawing the dreamer's attention to a need for clarity in a situation, or it can be an assurance of protection. Who is keeping an eye on you?

Cosmetics

Cosmetics or make-up in a dream, can be alluding to a need to improve your image, or it can be a pun as in, to make-up with someone, with whom you have had a falling out.

Water

ater in a dream symbolises the emotional life of the dreamer and how successfully they deal with situations.

Drowning in a dream indicates that we are being overwhelmed by our emotions and unable to deal with them.

Swimming with ease, suggests that we are touch with our emotions and deal with them appropriately.

A river symbolises the river of life and being in touch with what we are meant to be doing.

Crossing a river indicates changes coming into the dreamer's life.

A lake indicates the spiritual and intuitive life of the dreamer.

Diving into water can represent going down into the subconscious.

Deep water suggests being out of one's depth.

Going down into water can suggest a renewal of one's strength, while coming up can suggest a new beginning.

Fountains in a dream can refer to your intuition and protection from the Great Mother.

The sea or ocean represents the collective unconscious and the availability of unlimited knowledge and information.

Stormy waters indicate stormy emotions and problems, while calm waters indicate peaceful times ahead.

Drinking water can suggest nourishment on an emotional or spiritual level, as in the water of life.

Bathing in water suggests purification.

Snow in a dream represents frozen emotions.

Reptiles

Reptiles in dreams represent the lower, more frightening energies of the personality that need to be controlled, or we can be devoured by them. It can also represent someone who is cold blooded about getting their needs met. Who in your life needs to exercise more self discipline, or who has lost the loving aspect of their personality?

Money

To find money in a dream indicates changes around you which despite small worries, will bring much happiness. To find gold indicates finding the gold within and indicates that your superior skills will put you ahead of your competitors. To find jewels indicates brilliance that will ensure swift elevation.

AWAKEN

To wake up in a dream, indicates becoming more spiritually aware, just as being asleep in a dream is an indication of being unavailable on some level. Is there someone in your life who is unavailable to you?

FIRE

F ire in a dream can represent change that is beneficial, as long as the dreamer does not get burnt.

The hearth fire represents a passionate and loving relationship in the home, just as cold ashes in the fire place indicate the end of a passionate relationship. How brightly does your flame of passion burn?

house

A house in a dream usually represents the dreamer, or perhaps is giving the dreamer insight into someone else's house or personality. How well maintained is your house and what does it tell the world about you? A childhood home in a dream can represent lessons we still need to learn, or it can be referring to suppressed emotions that were not adequately dealt with, at the time of the particular childhood trauma.

The different rooms of the house represent different aspects of the dreamer.

The garage is a place where tools are kept and so dreams about a garage are drawing attention to the skills we have already mastered and how we are using them.

The basement represents the unconscious and feelings and emotions that we may have repressed.

The hallway is where we meet and greet people.

The sitting-room represents our social life and a sofa represents a relationship.

The kitchen is the nourishing aspect of our personalities and how we nourish others.

The type of kitchen is important.

One friend, who was having relationship problems had dreamed of a commercial kitchen that was now closed.

He could see a list of names pinned to the wall and his was nearly at the bottom of the list.

Obviously his relationship had never been a loving relationship for his partner, only one of convenience and his needs were not high on her list of priorities.

The bedrooms of a house represent the relationships we have on an intimate level such as family.

The beds are also significant. A single bed indicates a single person and a double bed representing a relationship with a partner.

The bath-room is where we cleanse ourselves of negative attitudes to a situation.

Using a toilet indicates emotional control and dealing with issues at the appropriate time and in the appropriate place.

It has been suggested that how we were toilet-trained as children has an impact on our attitude to money.

Perhaps constipation in our lives relate to a fear of money.

The attic of a house is where we store our memories of the past and sometimes we need to revisit certain memories before we can move forward.

Ceilings in a house represent the way we think about a situation as does the roof of a house.

ROOF

The roof is an important symbol of protection for the way the dreamer is thinking, so a dilapidated or damaged roof, suggests that caution needs to be taken because of a possible error of judgement on the part of the dreamer.

TREE

A tree in a dream can refer to you and your family tree, or to the tree of life and how you manage your opportunities for success. It may also refer to the amount of support you are getting from significant others. To climb a tree can indicate swift elevation in your chosen field, just as falling out of a tree can indicate that you have sabotaged you opportunities in some way. Pay attention to the details and health of your tree.

The trunk of the tree can represent how strong and self confident you are as an individual.

Any blemishes on the trunk can represent difficulties or heartaches experienced while growing up.

A broken branch can represent a death.

When I was married, I had a dream in which a massive branch broke off a tree and crashed down on the head of a young man, knocking him to the ground.

I told my husband about the dream the next morning and his immediate reaction was, "You think that is me!"

To which I replied, "I know that is you!"

I told him that the dream was a warning about the devastating effect his mother's death would have on him and that he would never recover from her death, because of their unbelievably close ties.

The size of the branch was a testimony to the huge influence that his mother had on his life and the tremendous force of the fallen branch on his head, indicated the effect her death would have on his attitude to life thereafter.

Sadly this warning did prove to be true.

Branches on a tree can represent opportunities and directions to go in.

Leaves can represent energy.

I had seen autumn leaves lying on the ground in a dream, when a young man I used to teach was dying of cancer.

Two weeks after the dream, the young man sadly passed away.

A strong root system on a tree can represent how grounded we are and how stable and secure we feel.

Mobile Phone

A mobile phone in a dream, like pen and paper, represents communication. A problem with mobile reception could indicate difficulty with self expression and a failure to be properly understood.

EXPLOSION

An explosion in a dream can represent a release of negative emotions that can have a destructive effect on relationships. Forewarned is forearmed, be careful of emotional outbursts after a dream of this nature.

SINGING

To sing in a dream indicates that we can raise our own vibration and the vibration of others. To hear others singing indicates pleasing companions and enjoyment of life.

Car

Driving a car in a dream indicates being in charge of a situation, but being a passenger indicates that someone else is in charge of what is happening. Position in the car is important, as it indicates personal power and status. The type of car in the dream is also significant, and provides more information about the message being conveyed to the dreamer. Is it a sports car, a family car or an industrial vehicle?

To have a flat tyre can indicate a lack of energy on the part of the dreamer and the position of the tyre is important.

The right side of the car is how we are thinking about a situation, the left side our intuition.

The Back wheels can represent how we are moving out of our past experiences.

SPIDERS

Spiders in a dream can be disturbing but need not symbolize bad luck. If a spider bites you in a dream, it can indicate that you are caught in a web of lies, but to see spiders in webs indicates favourable conditions. To see one building its web indicates a secure and happy home.

ḣeⱯRT

The heart in a dream usually refers to the emotional state of your heart. Are you frightened of getting hurt, or are you frightened of showing your emotions? The context of the dream is important, but if in doubt and you do have a physical heart problem, seek medical advice.

ROAD

A road in a dream indicates how we are progressing through life. A bend in the road alerts us to an unexpected happening. A road going up a hill indicates the amount of effort needed to complete our journey, while a straight road indicates that the path we are on is straight forward.

Back yard

To dream of the back-yard of a house is alerting the dreamer to situations from the past being repeated in the present. Learning how to deal appropriately with these situations is being highlighted for the dreamer. A familiar back yard will shed light on the type of experience that needs to be addressed.

An example of this is the dream of one young man who had a dream in which he found himself in his grandmother's house.

When he went into the backyard of his grandmother's house he turned into a Black Panther and in the back-yard he saw a pride of Lions that, although not openly aggressive, made him feel nervous.

The Lions then began climbing all over him and he was having trouble getting them off, as they were becoming more forceful in their attention.

Eventually, he managed to free himself and climb up a through a manhole in the ceiling and he just disappeared from view.

A simple way of looking at this dream in the context of the dreamer is as follows.

The dreamer is a young man who is extremely intuitive and comes from a cultural background where the male partner is always considered to be in the right.

This is symbolized by the Black Panther, a big cat of indisputable intuition and one of the animals at the top of the food chain.

The Black Panther also taps into the shadow side of the young man's nature and his intuitive ability, which can be used for a sense of power over others.

In this case his partner, who is born under the sign of Leo, and is represented by the lions.

The back yard represents issues from the past that are still affecting their relationship and causing conflict between them, as seen by his fear of the lions overpowering him and his eventual escape through a manhole in the ceiling, manhole being a pun for a male attitude to the situation, which stops any further discussion by being unavailable to his partner.

The ceiling in the dream represents the mind and how he is thinking.

The reference to the back-yard of the house of his grandmother is in effect the Wise Old Woman of Carl Jung's Collective Unconscious.

It is in fact a nurturing aspect of the young man's own personality and its higher perspective of what is causing a problem in his relationship.

Individuals, who have been fortunate enough to have a close relationship with their grandparents, will often find their grandparents in their dreams as a substitute for the Wise Old Man or Wise Old Woman of Jungian psychology.

Ԧɑɪʀ

To have your hair cut in a dream indicates that symbols of vanity are being taken from the dreamer. To dream of having your hair coloured by a hairdresser, indicates that a timely change in you expressed intentions, will save the dreamer from the scorn of others. Hair falling out in a dream and baldness apparent, indicates that the dreamer will have to earn their own living, as fortune has passed them by.

Golden hair in a dream indicates someone who will never behave badly towards another. Red hair in a dream suggests changes which often bring sadness.

If the hair turns white overnight in a dream, while the face remains young, an easy passage through life for the dreamer is indicated.

An abundance of healthy, well kept hair indicates happiness and abundance.

To cut your hair close to the scalp and baldness apparent indicates that generosity to others has left the dreamer in dire straits financially.

To have your hair cut in a dream also indicates serious disappointments.

Tangled and unkempt hair indicates that life will be a burden both in business and in the home.

To see oneself covered with hair indicates a person who considers themselves above the law and is only interested in satisfying their own pleasure.

Hair can also represent strength and virility as in the bible story of Samson and Delilah.

Certain cultures frown on a male child's hair being cut, before the age of five.

Toad

A toad in a dream indicates that the dreamer is being alerted to something ugly in his behaviour and the possibility of change. Like the frog in a dream, transformation is possible. Are you or is someone you know, resentful or jealous of another and so behaving badly?

Bus

Being on a bus in a dream indicates that what is happening around the dreamer is in the interests of a particular group as a whole. Position in the bus is important. Are you in the back seat, or are you at the front where you can see exactly what is going on? Getting off the bus indicates that you are now leaving a situation, where you were part of an effort, with a common goal.

Shoes

Shoes in a dream are significant of how grounded we are in our lives and how financially secure we are. The type of shoe and the colour of the shoe are both significant.

Sensible walking shoes indicate long term security. Soles coming off the shoes indicate a loss of income and possibly a loss of employment. High heels indicate a position of status, the higher the heel, the higher the status. Casual sports shoes can indicate a too casual approach to life, if they are seen in a dream in an inappropriate context. Or, sports shoes can indicate how well we play the game of life.

Laughing

To laugh in a dream suggests enjoyment of friendships and life in general, unless there is a discordant note in the dream. Care should be taken after such a dream. An old saying is "Them that laughs silly, will cry before night" is well worth keeping in mind.

LADDER

To ascend a ladder in your dream indicates progress in your life through personal effort.

Horse

A horse in a dream relates to the power within the dreamer. To ride a horse that is saddled and bridled indicates being fully in control of a situation. To ride a horse bare back indicate that only after hard struggle, will ease and comfort be obtained.

A white horse represents feminine power. A black horse represents commercial success and a brown horse indicates being committed to a situation.

Taxi

To be a passenger in a taxi indicates that the dreamer is being given a helping hand.

HALLWAY

The hallway is where we meet people. A light in a hallway indicates insight into the personality of the people we meet, just as an ill lit hallway is a warning to be careful of those you are about to encounter. Switching of a light in a hallway can also indicate the conscious termination of a relationship.

Sex

To be having sex in a dream indicates that the dreamer is becoming closer on an emotional level, to their partner. Phallic symbols in a dream however, may be drawing the dreamer's attention to the type of energy one produces.

A friend had a dream in which he was informing someone that he had, clear quartz, crystal penis.

As clear quartz amplifies the energy of other crystals, the dream was indicating that like clear quartz crystal, he is able to use his masculine energy to amply the energy of others.

Indeed a few days later, he was informed by the coordinator of a woman's group where he helped out, that the old ladies in the group really enjoyed his input, into their discussions and activities.

His assertive masculine energy was a tonic to their collective feminine energy.

Freud was quoted as saying that women suffered from penis envy, but the feminists claimed that it was the power of the penis that women envied, as in the masculine ability to command higher wages and greater status in the market place, not the penis itself.

Dream Example

To understand the symbolism of a dream, we need to ask ourselves if the dream is merely relating to the events of the previous day and providing deeper insight into the happenings and feelings of the day, or is there another message in the dream?

Is there perhaps insight into what is necessary to heal, or solve a problem in our lives?

One young man, who had a falling out with his partner, had a dream where he and his partner were going to take over a very dilapidated Pizza franchise, which they were going to do up. He said the building was in a very bad state of disrepair and would need a lot of attention, but he and his partner were determined to make a go of it.

While they were doing it up, someone arrived asking for a cup of coffee, only to be told to come back in twenty minutes, as the shop was not yet ready to be opened.

The dream illustrated that the young man needed to work hard on his relationship, as the dilapidated Pizza place, represented the lack of maintenance he had been putting into his relationship in recent months, which had resulted in the breakup of his relationship.

The determination to rebuild the Pizza franchise boded well for the future success of the relationship, as well as the willingness to put in the effort needed.

The customer, who wanted the cup of coffee, may indicate

someone who is curious about what has happened in the relationship, as coffee in a dream can represent gossip.

The time factor of twenty minutes can represent the relationship, as in 2 and two people and the zero may represent the female in the relationship, who had left, but it may also represent the time frame necessary for a healing of the relationship to begin.

Remember, man's time is not God's time, so twenty minutes could indicate twenty days, before a resolution to the situation.

The customer indicates that questions were being asked about what had happened, but the young man was not yet ready to answer them.

This dream revealed what was necessary for this relationship to heal and be successful.

As dreams can and often do, reflect something that was on our minds at the time of the dream, it is necessary to see how it might relate to some event, or preoccupation of the past day or two, or even week or two.

That is another reason why it is important to keep a record of daily events at the back of this book, so that one can cross reference information.

Dreams will throw insight into behaviour that we ourselves are refusing to look at.

A whole new dimension of wisdom and insight is added to our lives, which create a happier and healthier mental outlook, when we take the time to reflect in-depth, the meaning of our dreams.

Our dreams encourage us to stop drifting through life by revealing hidden talents and offering visions of what it is possible for us to achieve if, we put in the ground work necessary.

One young lady's dream of not having a train ticket, indicated that she had not yet achieved the necessary competence in her career to warrant the expectations that she held about future opportunities.

A train indicates a fixed route in our lives, something that is meant to be. Not having a ticket indicates that we are not well enough prepared, or we have not put in the necessary effort represented by the ability to pay for a ticket.

COLOUR

Dream Examples

I often hear people say that their dreams are only in black and white.

This can indicate a black and white attitude to life, or else the person may be unaware that we are all capable of dreaming in colour and so have accepted black and white as the norm in a dream.

Colours in dreams can give insight into the personality or motivations of a particular person.

Traditionally the colours of the earth relate to people born under the astrological signs of Taurus, Virgo and Capricorn but there are always the exceptions to every rule.

These are usually warm hearted, sociable individuals who are often referred to as, the salt of the earth.

These individuals are also well grounded in the material world and as a rule, reap the benefits of their hard work.

The warm autumn hues of greens and browns, yellows and oranges are frequently the preferred colours worn by these individuals and can often be used by the dreaming mind to illustrate a point that the dreamer needs to be made aware of.

Being an Aries fire sign and with a preference for cool colours of Spring, I had a dream in which I was surprised to find myself buying an orange dress, a colour more suited to an earth sign.

The next day I was amused to find myself purchasing a large

print that portrayed a lady in an autumn green dress, and who had orange hair which was the same colour as the dress which I had bought in my dream.

The dream seemed to suggest that I needed to be more grounded and practical, as well as more sociable in my life and provided a means to have a visual reminder.

Also, being a typical fire sign that rushes in and rushes out of situations, the earthy colours of autumn encourage me to take my time and pay more attention to detail.

In contrast, when the colour black is the preferred colour in a dream, the dreamer might be being alerted to a materialist disposition, or a preoccupation with the more materialistic side of life, or simply being shown the predisposition of another person's nature.

Contrary to negatives attitudes towards the colour black, it is an important indicator of financial acumen in dreams, although when combined with white, can indicate the black and white attitude of the dreamer.

Materialism is essential in our lives to ensure that we pay our bills and maintain a satisfactory life style and it is only when our lives become too materialistic, that the dreaming mind may challenge the dreamer's behaviour, through particular dream symbolism.

The colour of turquoise in a dream indicates how liberated the dreamer has become in different areas of their lives.

One dream a young woman had, in which she was wearing a turquoise top with white pants, indicated how liberated she was in the romantic and mothering aspect of herself, indicated by the turquoise top covering her breasts, while at the same time indentifying grief or sadness, regarding gender issues, symbolised by the white pants covering her legs.

The limbs usually refer to gender issues.

White can represent grief or sadness and to walk with a person who is wearing white indicates an awareness of a person's illness.

Red in a dream, if a mid red colour can represent standing in your personal power and sexuality, but fire engine red indicates anger.

Red can also indicate someone in your life who is a fire sign.

One dream a friend had about a huge red octopus pinning her down in shallow water, forewarned her about an angry emotional outburst by her partner, a ruling 8 in numerology, symbolised by the eight legs of the octopus.

The shallow water indicated that the anger was not deep seated anger, but just a flash of anger over something unimportant.

Numbers

Numbers in dreams also have particular meanings and may be alerting us to the type of opportunity available to us in our waking lives, or can represent a time frame for the accomplishment of a task, or an important meeting.

Also a play on words such as –Your number is up, in other words your time is up, or getting caught out in some way.

In numerology, a person's value system relates to their ruling number and so in dreams, we can often identify a person by what age they appear to be in the dream.

For example, to see a five year old child can represent someone who is a ruling 5 in numerology.

And then again, it can represent someone who is being childish. Dream context is important.

When I have a dream, I look at who the person in the dream might remind me of.

If I see someone who reminds me of my son in my dream, I know that it is usually referring to a person who either, has the same astrological sign as my son, or who has the same Chinese animal, or who has the same ruling number.

When I had a dream of English King, Henry the eighth, I knew my dream was referring to a friend who is a ruling 8 number.

Dreams always include symbolism that the dreamer can relate to.

Through an awareness of a multitude of symbolic meanings, we greatly enhance the richness of the dream landscape and provide ourselves with more opportunities to correctly understand and interpret our dreams.

ᗯᗩLL

A wall in a dream can represent boundaries, an obstacle, or support depending on the context of the dream and the circumstances of the dreamer at the time of the dream.

hotel

An hotel in a dream can represent a transient state in the dreamer's life or if working in a hotel, the dream could be making the dreamer aware that an improvement in financial opportunities needs to be addressed and that other opportunities are available.

MOUNTAIN

To climb a mountain in a dream indicates that you are making progress in your life. The effort needed, will correspond to the effort needed in waking life.

ꞶIND

Ꞷind in a dream usually corresponds to intellectual thought, but can also be attributed to spiritual influence in the dreamer's life. Circumstances at the time of the dream will clarify the situation.

How strongly the wind is blowing in a dream, is an indication of how passionate someone might be about a situation, where as a gentle breeze may symbolize encouragement for the dreamer.

Body Weight

Dream Example

Body weight in a dream is an indication of how well nourished we are emotionally and spiritually.

To be overweight in a dream, is an indicator of a self indulgent attitude by the dreamer, whilst to be underweight, points to a lack of emotional, or spiritual support in the dreamer's life.

A few years ago when I needed to defend my reputation against the lies and manipulation of the Principal of the school that I was teaching in and the unscrupulous manipulation of the facts, I had the following dream.

I dreamed that I was sitting on the toilet and I was only a skeleton and I could see a little round hole, the size of a twenty cent piece, in the outside wall on my left and through which I could see daylight.

I said to myself in the dream, "You are an ugly little girl but you are all I've got."

This dream on one level connected with the Irish Sheila-na-gig, a representative of the Goddess found on the corner stone's of the old Irish churches.

She is a naked old woman, who squats holding open her vulvae and offers protection to all. Similar carvings are found in old Churches across Europe.

On another level it was making me aware, that by going to the bare bones of the situation I found myself in, in other words making all the nitty gritty parts public, I was being viewed by others in an unflattering light, but it was also confirming that I had no one else giving me support.

The old adage, "If I am not for me, who is?" springs to mind here.

The small hole in the wall, through which I could see daylight, indicated that what I was doing, though unpopular, would eventually help me to break through obstacles, represented by the wall.

The symbol of being on the toilet represents using correct legal procedures to disclose what was happening and in an appropriate venue.

To feel a heavy weight of something in a dream, is an indication of being weighed down by your sense of responsibilities, or issues from your past.

To feel that your burden is light indicates that you will have no problems dealing with something.

My mother used to say that if you put your bundle of trouble down beside that of everyone else and you were asked to choose one, you would always choose your own bundle first.

HANDS

h ands represent the way in which we take hold of life.
Beautiful hands in a dream indicate the benevolence of
the individual towards others.

Blood on the hands can represent abuse of others.

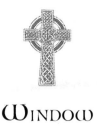

WINDOW

A window in a dream can represent the way we view the outside world, or it can be a pun as in a window of opportunity.

Looking in through a window can give you insight into a situation.

Door

Dream Example

A door in a dream can indicate the awakening of the dreamer to another aspect of their personality, which may offer insights into situations, or behaviour. It might even be a signal, that it is now the right time, for the dreamer to access a previously untapped inner resource.

It can also indicate a loss of opportunities, as in the case of one friend of mine who saw his white rabbit run out the front door.

In his dream, the rabbit knocked on the back door of the house and when he opened the door, the rabbit ran straight through the house and out the front door.

When he asked me what the dream meant I said his luck had just run out.

My friend then told me that his doctor had told him earlier in the week, that he had cirrhoses of the liver; a result of years of alcohol and drug abuse.

The seriousness of the situation only came home to him when he had the dream about the rabbit.

How many times do we believe that, "it will never happen to me" no matter how many warnings we are given?

The back door in the dream represented the past and the path of the rabbit to the front door, represented the path he had taken, which had resulted in his present health condition.

The symbolism of the front door was also a warning of the need to watch his health more carefully in the future.

Yoyo

A yoyo in a dream can represent opportunities around us that we are not taking seriously enough and so time runs out. Like the yoyo we go backwards and forwards and end up with nothing.

Other Animals in Dreams

Animals in dreams can be giving insight into a situation as in Chinese astrology.

A female dog with red fur in my dream, referred to an angry female born in the year of the dog.

Being bitten by a tiger snake in a dream can indicate an enemy born in the year of the tiger.

Monkeys in a dream can indicate deceit, or someone born in the year of the Monkey.

The twelve Chinese animals are important in interpreting dream messages and consist of; Rat, Ox, Tiger, Rabbit, Dragon, Snake, Horse, Goat, Monkey, Rooster, Dog and Pig.

When any of these animals appear in your dreams, it is advisable to think of the qualities attributed to these animals and that will give a good indication of the dream's message.

Wheat

To dream of a crop of any kind indicates success as in reaping the benefits of all your hard work.

JAIL

To dream of being in jail indicates that you feel your sense freedom is being restricted in some way.

The dream could be referring to your career or your home life.

hANDKeRChIeF

To dream of a handkerchief indicates grief, or that the dreamer may be feeling sorry for themselves

Death

To dream of the death of someone indicates the death of a particular relationship as we know it, whether personal or professional. For example, to get divorced is the death of a marriage. For someone to be murdered in a dream, indicates a violent emotional or psychological end to a relationship.

For an actual death to occur as a premonition, the dream may involve a funeral procession or a white bird that can be a harbinger of sad tidings, or other symbolic images.

Before my father-in-law died, I dreamed of an old scrawny grey cat coming through my bedroom wall towards me.

To dream of such a cat indicated his illness and warned me that he lay at death's door.

My son dreamed that he saw me in a hospital bed with tubes coming from my body and he saw a hospital chart on the wall behind my bed, with a zigzag line going across it recording my heart rate.

The dream however was about his grandmother, who had a cerebral haemorrhage a few weeks later and died in hospital.

We need to be careful when interpreting this type of dream as it can only be verified after an event and we need not give ourselves unnecessary anxiety.

Ship

To dream of a ship can be referring to the type of relationship that you are in.

When my marriage collapsed, I had a dream that I was now leaving a huge grey battleship.

My dreams tell me that my current relationship is a cruise ship.

What type of ship are you on?

Teeth

To dream of front teeth falling out, indicates that the dreamer is concerned about their appearance, or perhaps the aging process.

Back teeth represent family issues.

BIRDS

It is a favourable dream of birds with beautiful plumage, as it indicates that a wealthy and congenial partner is near.

Flying birds represent prosperity.

TOILET

T oilet dreams relate to how we deal with our emotions. If we are able to use a clean toilet, then we are dealing with unpleasant situations in a proper manner and in the appropriate place.

BIBLIOGRAPHY

Business Law of Australia; R.B. *Vermeesch* & K.E.*Lindgren* 5th Edition Butterworth's 1987

Butterworth's' Australian Competition Law; *Steinwall-Duns-McMahon-Narajan-Smith- Walker-Hurley*

Student Companions; Contracts *Matthew Smith* 1984
Sydney-Melbourne-Brisbane-Adelaide-Perth- Canberra-Hobart
Corporation Law; 4th Edition *Graeme Wiffen* 1997
Sydney-Adelaide-Brisbane-Canberra-
Melbourne-Perth
Torts; 5th Edition 1999 Duncan Holmes
Sydney-Adelaide-Brisbane-Canberra-Melbourne-Perth

Cases and Materials on Contract Law in Australia 2nd and 3rd Edition 1991 and 1998

J.W. *Carter* & D.J.*Harland*

Excel HSC Advanced English 2001/2002 and 2012. *Barry Spur and Lloyd Cameron*

Pascal Press

Intimidation Rituals: Reactions to Reform 1974 Volume 10 Number 3 *Rory O' Day*

University of Waterloo, Ontario Canada

Introducing Jung 1999 *Maggie Hyde* and *Michael Mc Guinness*

Law of Employment in Australia 1991

CCH Industrial Law Editors in Consultation with *Peter Punch*

CCH Australia

Litigation Evidence and Procedure 6th Edition 1998

Mark Aronson and *Jill Hunter*

Butterworth

Occupational Health and Safety Law in Australia 4th Edition *Adrian Brooks*

CCH Australia Limited

"If" by *Rudyard Kipling*

Magic, Its Ritual, Power and Purpose W.E. *Butler* 1952

Weatherby, Woolnough, Wellingborough

Northants, England

Paganism (a beginner's guide) *Teresa Moorey* 1996

Headway-Hodder&Stoughton

Shamanism (a beginner's guide) *Teresa Moorey* 1997

Hodder&Stoughton

The Law Handbook 9th Edition

Redfern Legal Centre Publishing 2004

Rosindubh: The Irish Dream Catcher *Rosemary Dawson* 2015

Balboa Press

The Law of Employment 4th Edition 1997 *James J Macken, Paul O' Grady, Carolyn Sappideen*

LBC Information Services

The Macquarie Easy Guide to Australian Law *Jan Bowen* 1992 The Macquarie Library

The Holy Bible New King James Version

Thomas Nelson Publishers Nashville

The Nostradamus Code *Ottavio* C *Ramotti*

Destiny Books division of Inner Tradition International 1998

The Sunday Telegraph

Timothy Winters by *Charles Causley*

Uniform Evidence Law *Stephen Odgers* 4th Edition1998

LBC Information Services 2000

Witta: An Irish Pagan Tradition 1993 *Edain McCoy*

Llewellyn's World Magic Series

1,000 Places to See Before You Die *Patricia Schultz* 2003

Epilogue

Certain poems resonate with the individual at particular times during their lifetime and the following poem by Rudyard Kipling, gave me the courage and determination to fight for truth and justice, despite the adversity of my situation.

I kept a copy of the poem in a prominent position beside my computer, so that I constantly glanced at it, as I went about my work.

It is important to have a source of inspiration that will motivate the individual and keep reminding them to stay on track.

If

"If you can keep your head when everyone about you is losing theirs and blaming it on you,

If you can trust yourself when all men doubt you, but make allowance for their doubting you,

If you can wait and not be tired by waiting, Or being lied about, don't deal in lies...................."

The next section of this book is provided as a little reminder for the reader to jot down the little happenings of the day.

Who?

What?

When?

Where?

Who?

What?

When?

Where?

Who?

What?

When?

Where?

Who?

What?

When?

Where?

Who?

What?

When?

Where?

Who?

What?

When?

Where?

Who?

What?

When?

Where?

Who?

What?

When?

Where?

Who?

What?

When?

Where?

Who?

What?

When?

Where?

Who?

What?

When?

Where?

Who?

What?

When?

Where?

Who?

What?

When?

Where?

Who?

What?

When?

Where?

Who?

What?

When?

Where?

Who?

What?

When?

Where?

Who?

What?

When?

Where?

Who?

What?

When?

Where?

Who?

What?

When?

Where?

Who?

What?

When?

Where?

Who?

What?

When?

Where?

Who?

What?

When?

Where?

Who?

What?

When?

Where?

Who?

What?

When?

Where?

Who?

What?

When?

Where?

Who?

What?

When?

Where?

Who?

What?

When?

Where?

Who?

What?

When?

Where?

Who?

What?

When?

Where?

Who?

What?

When?

Where?

Who?

What?

When?

Where?

Who?

What?

When?

Where?

Who?

What?

When?

Where?

Who?

What?

When?

Where?

Who?

What?

When?

Where?

Who?

What?

When?

Where?

NOTES

NOTES

NOTES

NOTES